Hill

Alternatives to Worksheets

Written by Karen Bauer and Rosa Drew

Illustrated by Gary Mouri

Edited by Janet Bruno

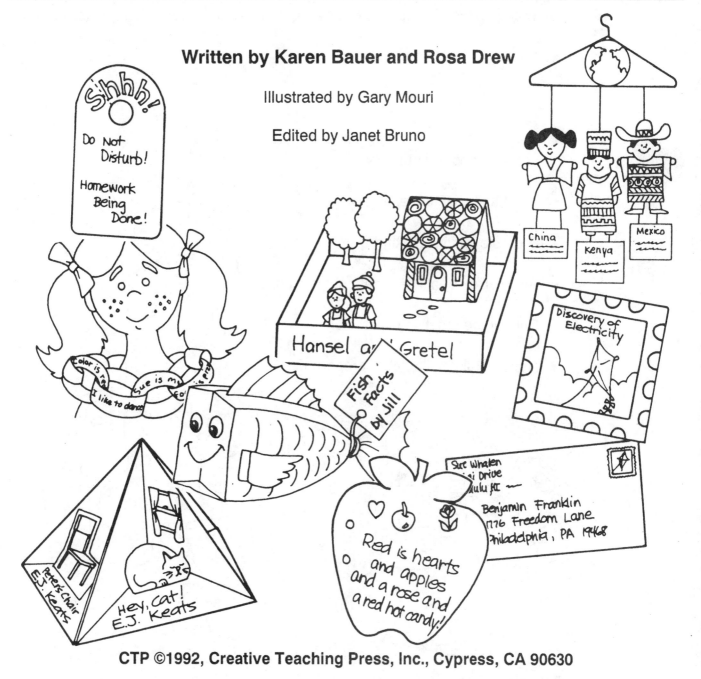

CTP ©1992, Creative Teaching Press, Inc., Cypress, CA 90630

Alternatives to Worksheets is just what every teacher needs—a resource book with hundreds of meaningful and motivating activities that students can work on independently. Now you and your students will never be at a loss for exciting and challenging projects.

A welcome change of pace from worksheets, these activities will raise student involvement to new levels and generate genuine enthusiasm for learning. You will love the imaginative alternatives described in this book and so will your students. These activities . . .

- Are adaptable to any theme

- Increase student involvement and motivation

- Require students to *apply* skills, not just circle answers and fill in blanks

- Emphasize written expression

- Promote critical thinking

- Allow all students to experience success

- Encourage creative expression

- Require minimal teacher preparation

Table of Contents

How to Use This Book

As you look through **Alternatives to Worksheets** you will find many new ideas, along with new twists on old favorites. Choose the project that best suits the needs of your class. The handy list of materials makes teacher preparation easy, and the illustrations help you see at a glance how to complete the project. The patterns you will need are at the back of this book.

Steps to Student Success

 When introducing a new activity to students, you may want them to begin the project as a whole group, then complete it independently. (Kindergarten teachers may find that young students need more direction from an adult.)

 The importance of teacher modeling cannot be overemphasized. When you carefully demonstrate and explain each step, your class will know how to proceed in order to complete a successful project. Students are then free to personalize and extend the activity according to their abilities.

 In preparation for the activity, have students brainstorm ideas in a large or small group. Brainstorming lets you find out what students already know about the topic and provides a pool of information that students can draw on as they complete their projects. Mapping, webbing, and making lists and word banks are common ways to brainstorm.

Grouping should be flexible. Students can work individually, with a partner, or in small groups. The activities in this book are especially appropriate for use at learning centers.

 A key element in each activity is a strong emphasis on writing. Younger students can rely on developmental (invented) spelling or dictate their writing ideas. Older students can move toward conventional spelling through the use of dictionaries and editing procedures.

 Students learn best when the same concept is presented in several different ways—so use a variety of activities for the same theme topic or concept. Also, don't hesitate to repeat an activity in different subject areas. When students know how to make the project, they can concentrate more on content.

Making It Your Own

Use this book as a resource and as a springboard for ideas. Personalize it by changing the activities to fit the needs of your class, and look for opportunities to apply the new formats to projects you have used in the past. ENJOY!

Accordion Books

Accordion books are a fun way for students to organize their work. A natural for sequencing activities, they can also be used by individuals or groups to display stories, poems, or factual information.

Materials:
- butcher paper, shelf paper, or construction paper
- crayons/markers
- writing paper
- glue
- pencils
- scissors

Directions:
Cut paper to the desired length. Fold paper in half lengthwise for greater strength. Then fold it into equal segments, accordion-style. If you wish, segments can be cut into special shapes and taped together.

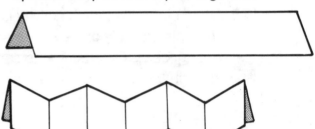

Class Books
Design a page with text and illustrations to contribute to a class accordion book on a chosen theme.

Step by Step
Illustrate and explain the steps necessary to complete a task. Be sure the steps are in the correct order.

Photo Album
Create your own album by drawing pictures related to a selected theme (pets, book characters, historical events) and writing about each one.

Alternatives to Worksheets   Creative Teaching Press

Postcards

Describe a trip you have taken by creating an accordion book of postcards showing trip highlights.

Science Growth Cycle

Illustrate and explain a growth cycle.

Holiday Book

Make an accordion book that reflects the special meaning of a holiday.

Retelling a Story

Write about, illustrate, and sequence the important events in a story.

Vertical Accordion Books

Accordion books can be made in a vertical format. All topics previously listed are suitable. Add a new twist by unfolding the book to show growth.

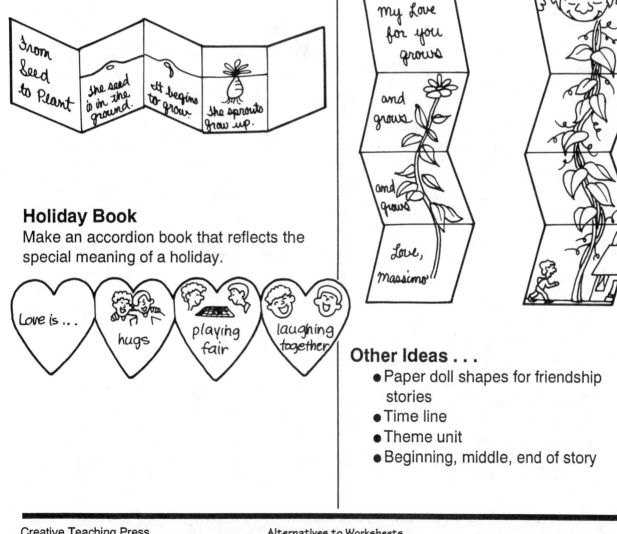

Other Ideas . . .

- Paper doll shapes for friendship stories
- Time line
- Theme unit
- Beginning, middle, end of story

Alphabet Books

Alphabet books can be used in all areas of the curriculum. They work well as class, group, or individual projects. The books' degree of difficulty can be adapted to meet the needs of your class.

Materials:
- paper
- pencils
- crayons/markers
- construction paper
- glue
- scissors

Directions:
Pick a theme for the book. Make a separate page for each letter of the alphabet. Write a word, sentence, or paragraph for each letter. Illustrate each page.

Thematic ABC Books
Look for words in an area of study which fit every letter of the alphabet.

Careers

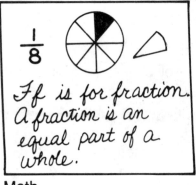

Math

Literature-Based ABC Book
Use words from favorite literature books that describe characters, plot, or setting.

Class ABC Book
Record interesting facts about your class.

Alphabet Nouns

Select a noun and use the shape of the first letter to illustrate it.

Alliterative ABC Book

Write a phrase or a sentence in which all the words begin with the same letter.

Action ABC Book

Select an action word. Illustrate it by making the first letter do the action.

Tactile ABC Book

On each letter, glue objects that begin with the letter.

Attribute ABC Book

Select a word that describes an object. Use the first letter of that word on the alphabet page.

Other Ideas . . .

- Country
- State
- All About Me, A to Z
- Weather
- Oceanography
- Adjectives from A to Z
- Famous Person ABC

Awards

Making awards encourages students to look for the unique qualities of a book, another person or themselves. Awards generate positive feelings in both the giver and the receiver.

Materials:
- construction paper
- pencils
- scissors
- crayons/markers
- pattern, p. 86 (optional)

Directions:
Have students design their own award or use the pattern on page 86. Awards can be made in a ribbon or certificate format.

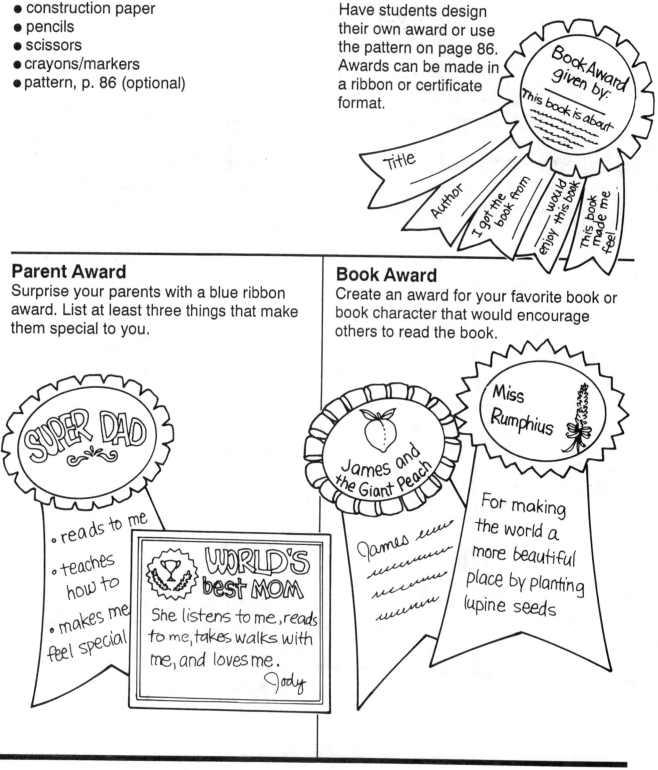

Parent Award
Surprise your parents with a blue ribbon award. List at least three things that make them special to you.

Book Award
Create an award for your favorite book or book character that would encourage others to read the book.

Alternatives to Worksheets

Creative Teaching Press

Historical Hero
Select a historical figure you admire. Design an award for this person.

Albert Einstein For producing the theory of relativity

Self-concept Award
Recognize your own special qualities by making an award for yourself!

I am doing great at learning to use the computer.

August Lobato (me)

School Worker Award
Create an award for a school employee who helps you during the day. Present the award and watch for a big smile.

Mrs. Beehler Cafeteria Manager

· Serves great food
· Patient
· Kind
· Always smiles

Friendship Award
Let your friends know how you feel about them or cheer them on for a job well done.

Bill is special because:
* He always hangs in there.
* He is creative.
* He is a friend to others.
* He likes me.

Mary Ann is a Super friend because

· She helps others.
· She makes me laugh.
· She is brave.
· She is clever and witty.

Other Ideas . . .
● Pet award
● Sibling award
● Achievement award
● First prize award
● Kindness award

Belts

Students love to exhibit their work. Give them an opportunity to display it in wearable form by making tagboard belts.

Materials:
- tagboard (3" x 20")
- yarn
- hole punch
- crayons/markers
- scissors
- pencils

Directions:
After students draw and write on the tagboard strip, punch a hole in each end and tie with yarn.

Parts of Speech Belt
Use verbs to tell what you like to do or adjectives to describe yourself.

Phonics Belt
Write and/or illustrate words that have the sound you are learning.

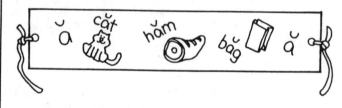

Story Sequence Belt
Use the belt to show the beginning, middle, and end of a favorite story.

Theme Belt
Illustrate and write about something you learned during the current theme unit.

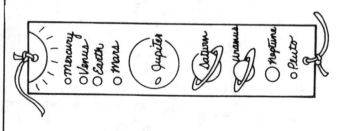

Time Line Belt

Make a time line showing historical events or important events in your own life.

Health Belt

Show ways to stay healthy on your health belt.

Pattern Belt

Make a belt that shows a pattern involving color, size, position, or shape.

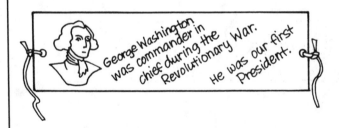

Number Belt

Practice writing your numbers by 1's, 2's, 5's, or 10's.

5, 10, 15, 20, 25, 30, 35, 40, 45, 50
55, 60, 65, 70, 75, 80, 85, 90, 95, 100

Famous Person Belt

Pick a famous person or a famous book character. Draw and write the person's special achievements or unique qualities.

George Washington was commander in chief during the Revolutionary War. He was our first President.

Other Ideas . . .

- Ecology belt
- Autograph belt
- Friendship belt
- Career belt

Bookmarks

Students will have fun designing a unique bookmark for use during a theme unit or literature study. A folding bookmark provides space for students to summarize stories, list related books, record new vocabulary words, and write facts.

Materials:

- construction paper strips (4" x 8")
- crayons/markers
- scissors
- pencils

Directions:

Students fold the paper in half lengthwise, draw an appropriate figure at the top, and cut around it. The selected writing assignment is completed inside the bookmark.

Genre Bookmark

Make a bookmark that reflects the kind of books you enjoy reading. List the book titles and authors inside.

Book Characters

Design a bookmark that represents a character in a favorite story. Write the book's title and author on the front. Inside, write about your character's admirable traits.

Alternatives to Worksheets

Creative Teaching Press

Famous Person

Before reading a book about a famous person, make a bookmark showing the head of the person at the top. On the inside, note important events in the person's life.

Theme Bookmark

Create a bookmark for the theme you are studying. On the inside, list facts you have learned.

Detective Word Search

Be a word detective. As you read your book, hunt for words that are new to you and write them inside the bookmark. Then look up their meanings and pronunciations in the dictionary.

Gift Bookmark

Design a bookmark for a friend or relative that reflects the person's interests. List this person's attributes or write a poem about him/her inside the bookmark.

Other Ideas . . .

- Note-taking bookmark
- Favorite quotes bookmark
- Poetry bookmark
- Talking bookmark

Box Activities

Boxes can be used for a wide variety of creative projects related to literature studies, theme units, and research activities.

Materials:
- boxes (shoe, shirt, cereal)
- tempera paint
- paintbrushes
- construction paper
- glue
- pencils
- crayons/markers
- scissors
- tape
- decorative paper (optional)
- butcher or shelf paper (filmstrip project)
- cardboard tubes or wooden dowels (filmstrip project)

Directions:
If students wish, they may paint or cover boxes with decorative paper in preparation for these projects.

Diorama
Build a scene inside or on top of a box, showing something you have learned in science, social science, or literature. Write about your diorama on a large index card and attach it to the box.

Shoebox Filmstrip
Cut a window in the bottom of a shoebox and slits in the sides. Cut butcher paper so it can be pulled through the slits. On the paper, draw pictures that will fill the screen. They can show a story sequence, an important event in history, a life cycle, or events in your life. After threading the filmstrip through the slits, secure each end to an empty cardboard tube.

Cereal Box Book

Paint the cereal box. When it is dry, decorate the box to resemble the cover of a book. Write facts about the book and glue them on the back.

Shoebox Book Float

Turn a shoebox upside down and use construction paper to create a scene from a favorite book. Line up the book floats for a classroom parade of literature.

Peek Box

Select a setting from social science or literature. Color and cut out objects for the scene, leaving a tab at the bottom of each to glue to the bottom of the shoebox. Cut a peek hole in the end of the box and one in the lid. Write a paragraph about your scene and attach it to the lid of the box.

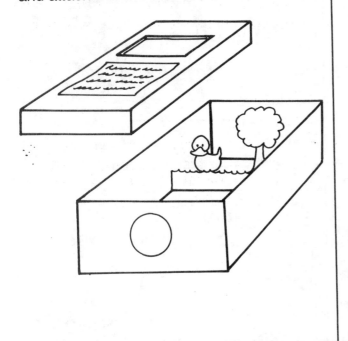

Box Animals

Using a box for a body and a stuffed paper bag for a head, create an animal from science or literature. Add details made from construction paper scraps. Write facts about your animal on paper cut to fit the box.

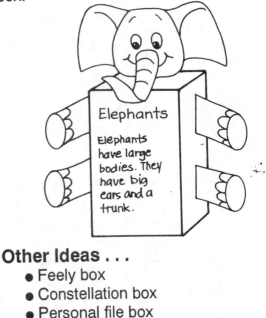

Other Ideas . . .
- Feely box
- Constellation box
- Personal file box
- Mailbox

Buttons and Bumper Stickers

When students design buttons and bumper stickers, they learn to get their message across in as few words as possible. Students think creatively as they play with words and phrases, selecting those that best communicate their ideas. Students can use the back of the project to explain their ideas in more detail.

Materials:
- construction paper, 4-1/2" x 12" (for bumper sticker)
- tagboard circle, 3" (for button)
- crayons/markers

Directions:
Prepare paper for the selected project. Show the class sample buttons and bumper stickers.

Make a Statement
Design a button or bumper sticker that makes a personal statement. Write about it in more detail on the back.

Campaign Slogan
Write a slogan that will convince people to vote for you or a favorite candidate. On the back, tell why you or your candidate is the best person for the job.

Support a Cause
Design a bumper sticker to show your support for a cause that will make the world a better place. Encourage others to support the cause by listing your reasons on the back of the sticker.

Friendship
Design a button for a friend so others will know why your friend is special.

Alternatives to Worksheets Creative Teaching Press

"Ask Me" Button

Become a class expert with an "Ask Me" button. Write the question on the front and the answer on the back.

Health Hint

Create a slogan that will promote healthy habits. Explain the slogan on the back.

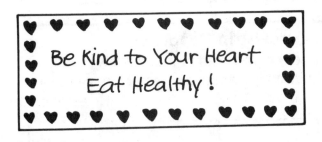

Self-esteem

Let everyone know you've done something well by making a button or a bumper sticker to broadcast the news!

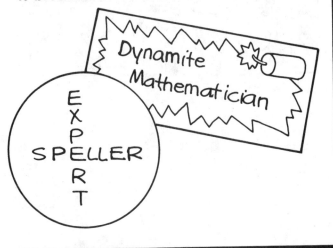

Team Literature

Working in teams of two or three, design a bumper sticker that gives a clue to a book the class has read. When all the bumper stickers are on display, work with your partner(s) to see how many books you can identify.

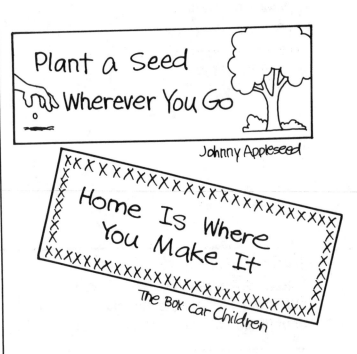

Other Ideas . . .

- Holiday announcements
- Historical events
- Science discoveries
- Special events

Cartoons and Comic Strips

Cartoons tell a story with pictures and a few well chosen words. They appeal to children of all grade levels and are an excellent vehicle for teaching students to write dialogue.

Materials:
- paper
- crayons/markers
- pencils

Directions:
Give students the opportunity to read single-frame cartoons and comic strips. Then have students create one of their own on a selected topic.

Literature
Write a conversation between two story characters. Explain the significance of the conversation on the back of the cartoon.

Comic Strip Report
Use a comic strip format to convey factual information about a selected topic.

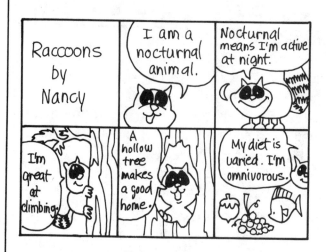

Sequencing

Use a comic strip format to show a sequence of events. Add your comic strip to a class collection, or cut the frames apart and have a classmate put them in order.

History

Draw a picture that includes at least two historical figures from a current unit of study. Write a conversation between them that reflects their period in history.

Self-concept

Draw a cartoon self-portrait and tell something about yourself. On the back of the cartoon, explain your thoughts in detail.

Health and Safety

Create a cartoon character to deliver a health or safety message.

Other Ideas . . .

- Original comic strip
- Support a cause
- Political cartoon
- Retell a favorite story

Chains

The strips of a chain visually emphasize the important parts of a whole idea. Concepts such as interdependence, life cycles, time lines, and parts of a whole become clear as the chains are assembled. Each student can make a chain or contribute one link to a class chain. Chains can also be hung as mobiles or worn as necklaces.

Materials:
- paper strips (approx. 3" x 12")
- crayons/markers
- glue or stapler
- pencils

Directions:
Decide on the topic and the type of chain (individual or class) you want to make. Have students write and/or draw information on the paper strips and assemble the chains using glue or staples.

Attributes
On each strip, write and/or illustrate important attributes of a person, place, or thing. Put the strips together to form a chain.

Time Line
Create a time line chain showing the order of events in history, your life, or the life of a famous person.

Alternatives to Worksheets   Creative Teaching Press

Facts

As you discover facts during a unit of study, write them on strips and add them to your chain.

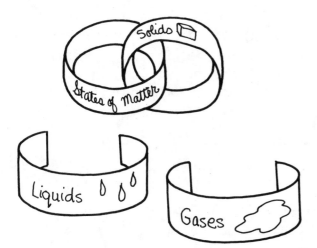

Literature

Use a chain to summarize a chapter or story, sequence story events, or review story elements.

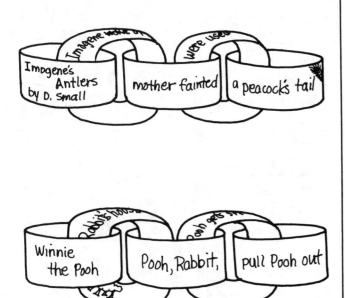

Life Cycles

Illustrate and write about a life cycle by using one link of the chain for each stage of the cycle.

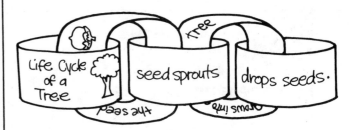

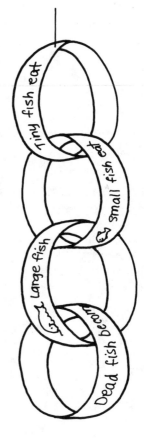

Other Ideas . . .

- Chain of books read
- Nutrition chain
- Pattern chain
- Math facts chain

Charts

Chart making is a practical way for students to organize information. When the charts are complete, students can compare and contrast the information charted or summarize and share what they have learned through discussion and writing.

Materials:
- paper (appropriate size)
- pencils
- rulers
- crayons/markers (optional)

Directions:
Have students decide on a horizontal or a vertical format for their chart. Then have them rule the chart into rows or columns, and add headings.

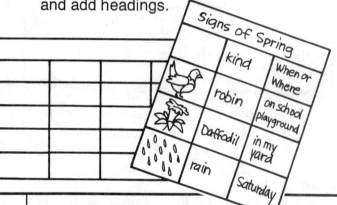

Social Science
Compare something in your culture with something from another culture. Write a paragraph about your findings.

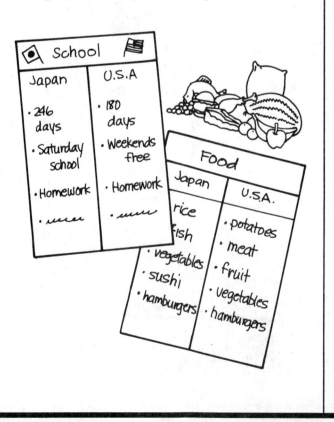

Word Search
Look for specific words or parts of speech on an assigned page in a book, magazine, or newspaper.

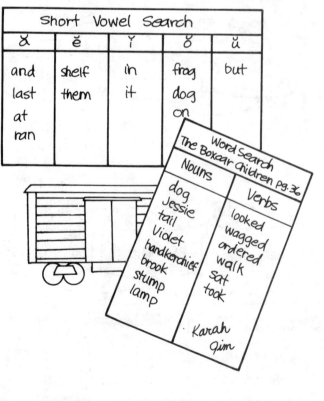

Plot Chart

Write or draw a picture showing the following elements of a story: characters, setting, problem, events, story ending.

Plot Chart				
Characters	Setting	Problem	Events	Ending
Frog/Toad	River	Toad didn't want to be seen in a swimsuit.	·Told frog ·Asked Animals to leave	·Toad came out of the water.

Author Study

After reading several books by one author, compare different aspects of the stories—setting, plot, characters.

Author: Leo Lionni		
Title	Main Character	Traits
Fish is Fish	Fish	Good Imagination Curious
Swimmy	Fish	Brave Leader
Alexander and the Wind-up Mouse	Alexander (real mouse)	Lonely True Friend

Theme Study

After reading several books on the same theme, chart the differences and similarities in plot, characters, and setting.

Theme: Dragons				
Title	Author	Main characters	character sketch	Plot
Everyone knows what a dragon looks like	Jay Williams			
Eyes of the dragon	Margaret Leaf	Painter	He paints dragons without eyes	
St. George and the dragon	Trina Schart Hyman			

Science

Make a chart comparing two or more things you are studying in your current science unit.

Dinosaur	Tyrannosaurus Rex	Triceratops	Brontosaurus
Traits	Ferocious		
Habitat	Land	Land	In or near water
Food	Meat	Plants	Plants
Special Features	Big Sharp teeth Walk on 2 feet	3 horns Frill on neck	Long neck and tail

Other Ideas . . .

- Families
- Historical figures
- Holidays
- Bad day/good day

Circle Activities

A basic circle is useful for many activities. This shape is a natural for life cycles, fractions, and circle stories.

Materials:
- construction paper, tagboard, or butcher paper
- circle pattern
- scissors
- glue
- crayons/markers
- pencils
- paper plates (for puppet)
- tongue depressors (for puppet)

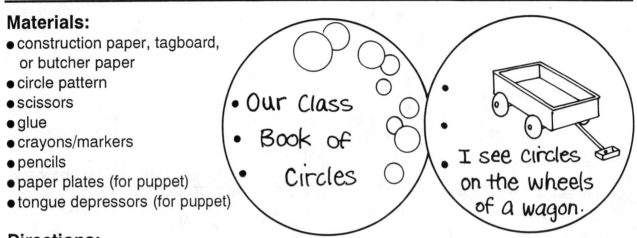

- Our Class
- Book of
- Circles

- I see circles on the wheels of a wagon.

Directions:
Cut circles of the desired size, have students trace a pattern and cut their own circles, or use paper plates for appropriate projects.

Phonics Hat
Cut out a 15" circle and fold it into fourths. Cut off one fourth of the circle. Decorate the remaining sections with pictures of, or words for, objects beginning with a given letter sound. Write the letter on the circle. Form the circle into a cone and staple.

3-D Dinner
Create a 3-D dinner with stand-up food to reflect concepts you have learned in literature, social science, or health.

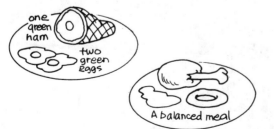

one green ham

two green eggs

A balanced meal

Life Cycles
Divide a paper circle or plate into four sections. Draw and label four stages of a natural cycle.

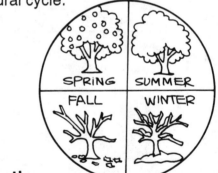

SPRING SUMMER
FALL WINTER

Fractions
Cut circles into different fractional parts and use the parts to make a picture. Write a description of what you have made.

Luis

Two ships are sailing.

Alternatives to Worksheets   Creative Teaching Press

Spirals

Cut a circle into a spiral. Write about the theme being studied on the spiral.

Circle Story

Write a story in a circle, starting in the center. Keep turning your paper and write your way to the edge.

Story Elements

Fold or divide a circle into fourths. Write the title and author in the first section. In the remaining sections, illustrate the beginning, middle, and end of a story. Write about each one.

Paper Plate Puppet

On the back of the plate, write about a character from literature or history. Draw and/or use scrap materials to make the front look like the character. Glue the plate to a tongue depressor. Use the puppet to tell the class about your character.

Group Story Pie

Working in a group of eight, cut a 36" circle from butcher paper. Divide it into eight equal sections and cut them apart. Write and illustrate your assigned part of the story on one of the sections. Assemble the pieces to make the story pie.

Other Ideas . . .

- Spiral notes or invitations
- Circle shape book
- Time line pie
- Character pie

Cubes

A six-sided cube encourages multiple responses to assignments. This, in turn, stretches student thinking and fosters creativity.

Materials:
- square boxes, milk cartons, or cube pattern, p. 87
- solid color butcher/wrapping paper
- tape or glue
- crayons/markers
- pencils

Directions:
Construct cubes from a square box of any size. Or trim two paper milk cartons to the same height and insert the open end of one carton into the open end of the other. Cover the cube with butcher paper or wrapping paper. Another option is to use the cube pattern on page 87.

Science
On each side of the cube, illustrate and label a science concept from a unit of study. Roll the cube and talk about or write facts about the picture shown.

Literature
Decorate a cube with the title, author, and five highlights from a story.

Math
Color dots on the cube to show the numbers 1–6. With a partner, roll two number cubes and add, subtract, or multiply the numbers that land face up. Write the number problems that are rolled.

Poetry

On each side of a cube, write or paste a copy of a poem. Roll the cube and recite the poem that lands face up. Illustrate the poem.

Social Science

Write and illustrate facts about a country you are studying.

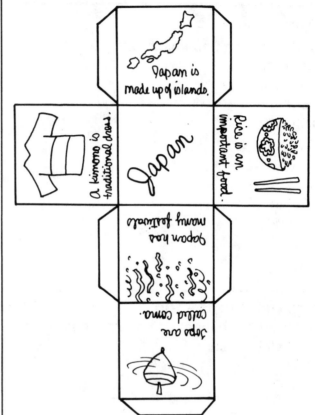

All About Me

Write your name on one side of the cube. Trace your handprint on another side. On the remaining sides, draw information about yourself.

Other Ideas . . .

- Shape cube
- Theme cube
- Cube city

Door Hangers

Door hangers offer students an opportunity to write brief messages to others and experience the excitement of delivery and discovery.

Materials:
- construction paper/tagboard
- scissors
- pencils
- crayons/markers
- pattern, p. 88

Directions:
Reproduce the pattern on page 88 or use it to make patterns for students to trace.

Factual Information
Make a door hanger listing information you are trying to learn. Place the hanger where you will see it each day.

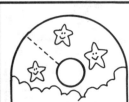

School Worker
Let your principal or someone else at school know why you appreciate him/her by writing your thoughts on a door hanger. Imagine that person's surprise and pleasure when the gift is discovered.

Friendship
Create a door hanger telling a friend how much you value his/her friendship.

Alternatives to Worksheets   Creative Teaching Press

Book Recommendation

Tell others about a book you think they would enjoy reading. Write your recommendation on a door hanger.

Do Not Disturb!

Make a "Do Not Disturb" door hanger to use when doing homework, reading, listening to music, or resting.

Invitation

Write a door hanger invitation asking another class to join in a special activity.

Reminder

Design a "reminder" door hanger for yourself. Place it on your bedroom door or inside the front door so you will see it as you leave the house.

Good News

Tell your parents some good news by writing it on a door hanger. Hang it on a door where they will be sure to see it.

Other Ideas . . .

- Notes to neighbors
- Delivery instructions
- Sorry I missed you
- Advertise an event

Envelopes and Stamps

Knowing how to address an envelope properly is an important life skill. Envelopes can be addressed and mailed, or make-believe addresses and stamps can be created to correlate with specific themes or units of study. This activity goes hand in hand with letter writing experiences.

Materials:
- envelopes or envelope pattern, p. 89
- plain paper or stamp pattern, p. 90
- crayons/markers
- pencils

Directions:
Using real envelopes or the pattern on page 89, instruct students in the correct procedure for writing the address and return address. Students can design stamps from squares of paper, or they can use the stamp pattern on page 90 to create giant stamps.

L. DeLucy
44 Mallard St.
Peking, FL 32751

National Wildlife Federation
8925 Leesburg Pike
Vienna, VA 22184 - 0001

Historical Figure
Address an envelope to a historical figure. Do research to find out where the person lived, then look up a current zip code for area. Design a stamp to honor the person or the event that made him/her famous.

Sue Whalen
6 Lai Drive
Honolulu, HI

Benjamin Franklin
1776 Freedom Lane
Philadelphia, PA 19468

Fictional Character
Address an envelope from one book character to another. Create an address, stamp, return address, and postmark that reflect the characters and the story setting.

Pig Three
10 Porker Lane
Hambone, MO

A. Wolf
c/o County Jail
Coyote Hills, WY 83001

Authors

Write a letter to your favorite author. Find out the name of his/her publisher and address the envelope appropriately.

Request Information

Address a business envelope for a letter requesting information or materials. Be sure to include your return address.

Support a Cause

Find the names of people in government or business who support a cause that you feel is important. Address an envelope to the person you select.

Design a Stamp

Design a commemorative postage stamp honoring a special person, animal, or place. Study real stamps to decide what information you should include on your stamp.

Other Ideas . . .

Address envelopes to:
- Classmates
- Famous living persons
- Friends
- Family

Flags

When students design a flag, they must capture the essence of a topic with symbolic illustrations and a few key words. Students should be given the opportunity to share their flags in oral or written form.

Materials:
- construction or butcher paper (assorted colors and sizes)
- writing paper appropriate to grade level
- glue
- pencils
- crayons/markers
- paper, cardboard, or stick flagpole

Directions:
Ask students to create or re-create a flag for the theme being studied. Then have students write about the topic and attach their work to the back of the flag. Glue the flag onto a pole.

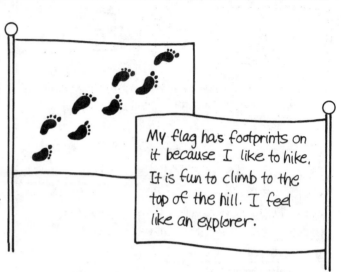

My flag has footprints on it because I like to hike. It is fun to climb to the top of the hill. I feel like an explorer.

Class Flag
Think of symbols that could represent your class. Create a flag that uses these symbols.

Author/Illustrator Flag
After researching the life of an author or an illustrator, create a flag that represents the person and his/her work.

Mrs. Bauer's Class

$\frac{4+2}{6}$

Mr. Burby's Team

In our class, everyone is a star. We all have good ideas to share.
Billy

DONALD CREWS

My flag for Jan Brett has animals on it because she likes animals. The flag has a border with a little picture just like hers.

Book Character Flag

Design a flag that represents a character from literature. Write about the character on the back.

Historical Flag

Make a flag that symbolizes a historical figure or event.

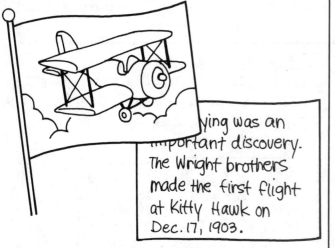

Geographical Flag

Re-create the flag of a city, state, or country. On the back, write facts about it.

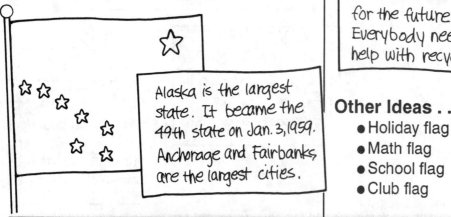

Personal Flag

Create a flag that tells others about you. Use the back of the flag to explain the symbols you chose.

Flag for a Cause

Make others aware of a personal concern by designing a flag that will enlist their support. Explain your concern in writing.

Other Ideas . . .

- Holiday flag
- Math flag
- School flag
- Club flag

Flaps

Flaps that lift to reveal what is underneath or inside give students the opportunity to make predictions and restate or review things they have learned.

Materials:
- construction paper (9" x 12")
- paper scraps (for flaps)
- writing paper
- scissors
- glue
- crayons/markers
- pencils
- pattern, p. 92 (for people)

Directions:
Select a project and determine the size of construction paper needed. Flaps can be made from scraps of paper and glued to the background along one edge only. Use the pattern on page 92 for the "People" project.

Riddles
Create flaps to conceal the answers to riddles on a current theme topic.

Literature Response
Illustrate your response to a story. Include at least one flap that conceals an important story idea. Write more about the story on the back of the paper.

People

Add a flap to the pattern on page 92 to reveal parts of the human body. Describe them on the back.

Use flaps to show people in different kinds of clothing such as ethnic costumes, seasonal outfits, and uniforms. Use the pattern on page 92.

Home Setting

Re-create your own home or a home from literature or history. Cut flaps in the top sheet for windows and doors. Illustrate the interior of the house on the bottom sheet of paper. Describe the setting on the back of the house.

Lincoln born in a log cabin. The floor was dirt. The fireplace was used for cooking and ....

Other Ideas . . .
- Greeting card
- What's inside?
- Riddles and answers
- Hidden clues

Flip-flaps

Flip-flaps are versatile, easy-to-make projects that offer the fun of manipulation and a hint of secrecy or surprise.

Materials:
- 12" x 18" or 9" x 12" paper
- scissors
- crayons/markers
- pencils

Directions:
Fold paper into eighths. Open and cut to center fold as shown. To create more flaps, fold and cut paper accordingly.

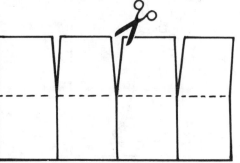

Science
Illustrate and write about a life cycle.

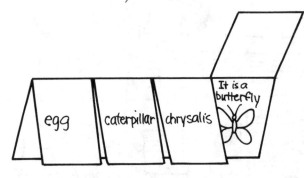

Literature
Illustrate or write about a story's main character, setting, problem, and solution.

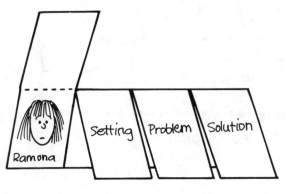

Following Directions
List the steps in a sequential project such as preparing a recipe.

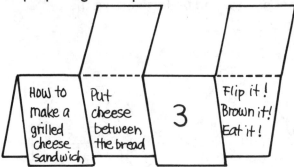

Math
Write a number on the top flap. Write facts for the number under the flap.

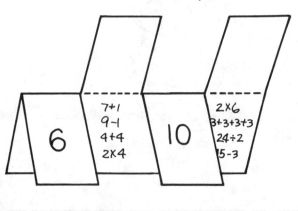

Alternatives to Worksheets Creative Teaching Press

Phonics

Write a different letter on each flap. On the inside, draw a picture beginning with the sound of the letter.

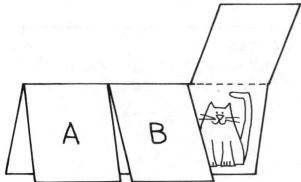

Riddles

Write a riddle on top and give the answer inside.

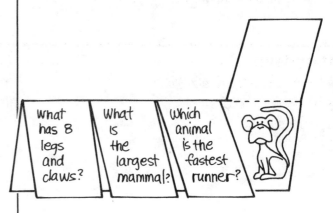

Character Descriptions

Draw the main characters in a story and list the attributes of each under the flaps.

Music

Draw music symbols and write their names under the flap.

Story Sequencing

Illustrate and write about the beginning, middle, and end of a story.

Other Ideas . . .

- Steps in an experiment
- Steps for building a project
- Ordering by size or number
- Mystery questions
- Clues and answers
- Synonyms/antonyms

Folded Paper Activities

Folded paper activities save teacher preparation time and provide students with an organized surface to work on.

Materials:
- plain paper (any size)
- crayons/markers
- pencils

Directions:
Instruct students to fold the paper according to the work they will be doing.

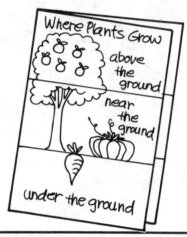

Halves
Use paper folded in half to compare and contrast people, places, or things.

Fourths
Fold paper in fourths to make a simple book for riddles, stories, or facts.

Outline story elements in each section.

Thirds

Use the three sections to compare and contrast two people, places, or things. List their similarities in the center section.

Ninths

Compile with the class a list of at least 15 words or facts on a given topic. Choose a different one to write about or draw in each section. Use the completed page in a game of bingo. (Note: The teacher or a student needs to make a set of calling cards for the complete list of words.)

Sixths and Eighths

In each section, draw and/or write according to teacher directions.

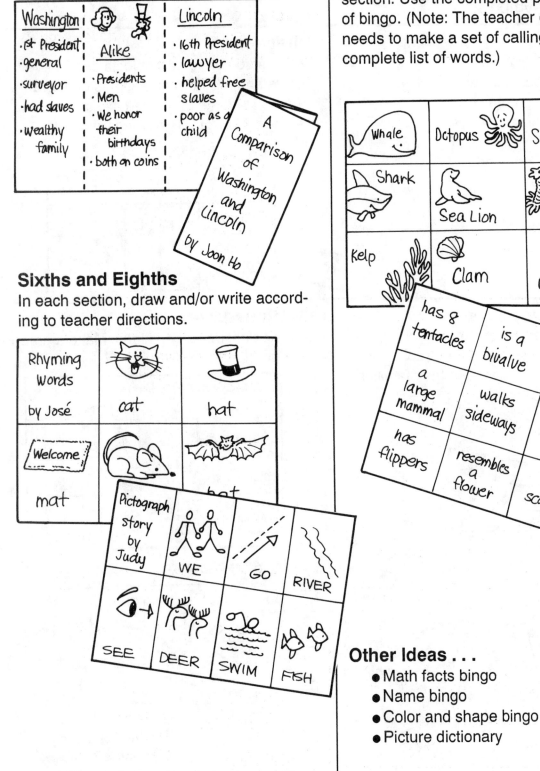

Other Ideas . . .

- Math facts bingo
- Name bingo
- Color and shape bingo
- Picture dictionary

Graphs

To make a graph students must gather, organize, categorize, and compare materials and information. When the graph is complete, students should be able to summarize the results in oral or written form. Graphing can be a whole class, small group, or individual activity and can be done with real objects, pictures, or symbols.

Materials:
- graph paper
- large sheet butcher paper (whole group graph)
- crayons/markers
- pencils
- objects to be graphed (if appropriate)

Directions:
Direct students to sort objects or to survey others and record their findings on a graph. At first, students may need assistance setting up the graph and recording the information.

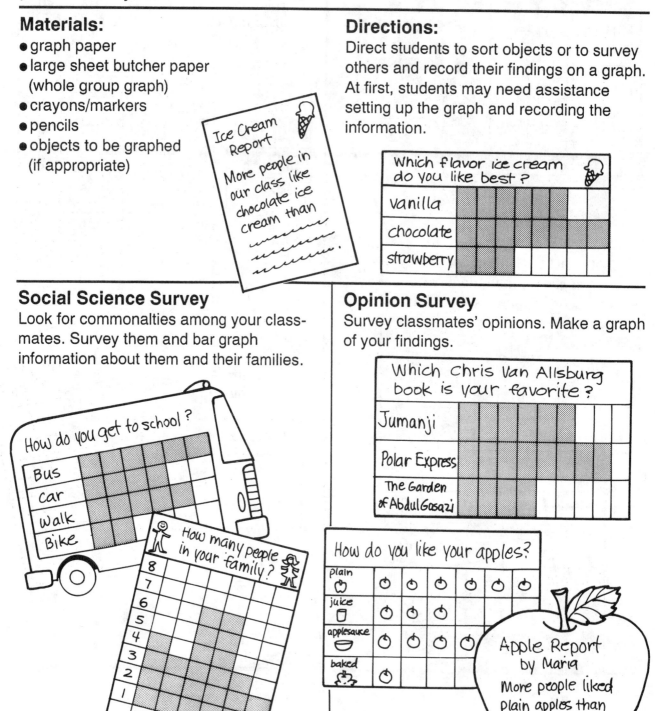

Ice Cream Report
More people in our class like chocolate ice cream than

Which flavor ice cream do you like best?
vanilla
chocolate
strawberry

Social Science Survey
Look for commonalties among your classmates. Survey them and bar graph information about them and their families.

How do you get to school?
Bus
Car
Walk
Bike

How many people in your family?

Opinion Survey
Survey classmates' opinions. Make a graph of your findings.

Which Chris Van Allsburg book is your favorite?
Jumanji
Polar Express
The Garden of Abdul Gasazi

How do you like your apples?
plain
juice
applesauce
baked

Apple Report by Maria
More people liked plain apples than juice or applesauce. Only one

Object Graphing

Sort the given objects by common attributes, graph the results, and compare your findings with those of others in the class.

Math Concepts

Use graphs to record findings about height/weight comparisons, probability, and other math concepts.

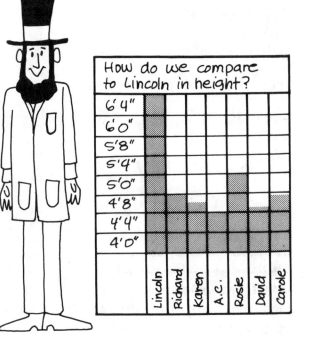

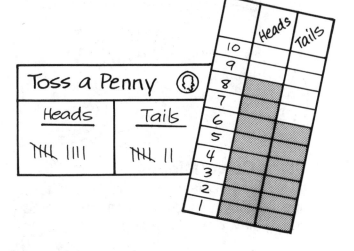

Other Ideas . . .

- Letters in your name
- Color of eyes/hair
- Favorite book character
- Favorites (on any topic)

Greeting Cards and Invitations

Writing greeting cards and invitations provides a meaningful way for students to practice written communication. In addition, designing and decorating the card offers opportunities for creative expression.

Materials:
- construction paper
- pencils
- crayons/markers
- scissors
- pop-up pattern, p. 91 (optional)

Directions:
Cut construction paper to the desired size. Students fold the paper in half and write a message on the card, adding appropriate illustrations. For the pop-up card, use the pattern on page 91.

Historical Figure Party
Select a historical figure and plan a party commemorating his/her contributions.

Class Celebration
Invite another class to join your class for a special activity, such as a reading celebration, a play, or a sing-along.

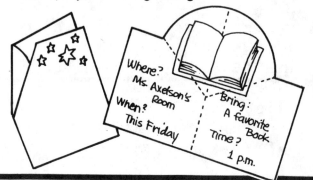

Author Birthday
Honor a favorite author's birthday by planning a classroom celebration.

School Event
Invite guests to a special school event.

Holiday Card

Send holiday wishes to someone special. Design the card around a holiday symbol.

Special Person Card

Create a personalized card to honor someone special. The message and decorations should reflect your feelings about the person and his/her unique qualities.

Get-Well Card

Cheer up a sick friend or a patient at a local hospital with an original card.

Storybook Party

Plan a party for a book character. Look in the story for things the character might like.

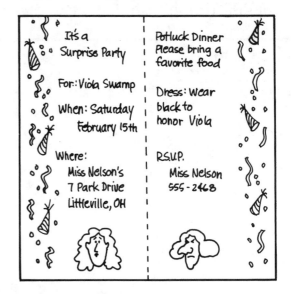

Special Event

Celebrate a special occasion by sending a personalized greeting card.

Other Ideas . . .

- Family/friend birthday card
- Mother's Day/Father's Day card
- Friendship card
- Open House invitation
- Back-to-School Night invitation

Journals

Making and keeping a journal is a good project for children of all grade levels. Journal writing encourages written fluency and the expression of thoughts and feelings. Younger students can draw pictures instead of writing journal entries.

Materials:
- writing paper
- construction paper or tagboard (for cover)
- pencils
- crayons/markers

Directions:
Staple several sheets of paper together for a simple journal, or bind paper into construction paper or tagboard covers. Use lined or unlined paper appropriate to your grade level.

Science Journal
Record science observations.

Prediction Journal
Predict what will happen and when. Then record the actual event and compare it with your prediction.

Personal Journal
Write about your thoughts and feelings.

Travel Journal

Write about real or imaginary travels.

Historical Journal

Pretend to be a historical figure and write about an important event in your life.

Literature Response Journal

Respond in writing to a story event or character.

Double Entry Journal

Select a quotation from a story. Write about a personal experience that relates to the quotation.

Buddy Journal

Team up with a classmate and write journal entries to each other.

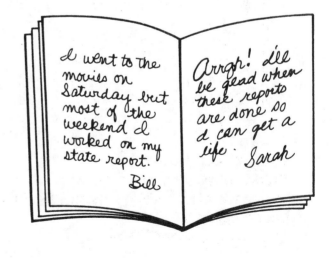

Other Ideas . . .

- TV response journal
- Nutrition journal
- Individual progress journal
- Theme unit journal

Letters and Notes

Writing letters and notes gives students a real reason to practice their writing skills. Children like to write letters and love to receive them. The type of letter—formal or informal—can be varied according to the teaching objective.

Materials:
- paper for stationery
- pencils
- crayons/markers (optional)

Directions:
Decide on the type of letter you want students to write and give directions accordingly. To personalize their letters, students can decorate or change the shape of their stationery.

Dear Karen,
It was fun to "pig-out" at lunch with you. I will call you soon.
Love, Rosa

Pen Pals
Write to someone in another class or at another school. Share your interests and ask questions your pen pal can answer in a return letter.

Dear Sue,
Thank you for the letter. It was good to hear from you.
We have been busy at our school, too. We are learning about dinosaurs. We are making fossils and digging them up.
What have you been doing?
Your Pen Pal,
Carole

Book Character
Write a letter or a note to a favorite book character. (Note: Arrange with an older class to answer the letters as if they were the book characters.)

Dear Toad,
I know you look forward to getting mail. I enjoy your adventures.
Janet

Dear Janet,
Your letter means a lot to me. I'm glad I have a frog for a friend to help me out!
Toad

Author

Write a letter to an author you especially enjoy. Tell why you like his/her stories and characters.

Dear Aliki,

Your books helped me learn about dinosaurs. How did you learn so much?

Mark

Fan Mail

What would you like to ask a famous person? Write a letter asking for this information.

5144 Michelson
Irvine, Ca 92715
September 19, 1991

President
White House
1600 Pennsylvania Ave.
Washington, D.C. 10...

Dear Sir,

Did you enjoy reading books when you were a child? What was your favorite book?

Sincerely,
Zenobia Blake

P.S. You're doing a good job.

Family

Write a letter or a note to a family member. Compliment the person on something he/she does well.

Dear Grandma,

You make good cookies. I love you.

Jeff

Historical Letters

Write a letter as a child in history. For example, pretend to be a Pilgrim on the *Mayflower* or a child going west in a covered wagon.

Dear Blue Feather,

Tomorrow my people will take down our homes and travel north, following the buffalo. Bright Sun

Requesting Information

Write to an organization requesting information on a subject you are studying.

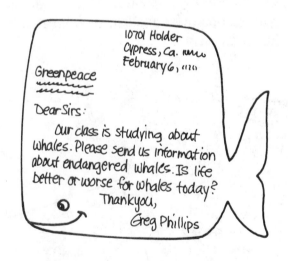

10701 Holder
Cypress, Ca. ....
February 6, 19...

Greenpeace

Dear Sirs:

Our class is studying about whales. Please send us information about endangered whales. Is life better or worse for whales today?

Thank you,
Greg Phillips

Other Ideas . . .

- Letters to senior citizens
- Get-well letters
- Letter to a classmate
- Letter from a historical figure

Lists and Checklists

Lists and checklists help students organize their thoughts and give them practice using key words to express ideas. Generating the list, prioritizing the entries, and checking off accomplishments bring closure to the task. Younger children can make lists by drawing pictures of the items they want to include.

Materials:
- plain or lined paper
- crayons/markers
- pencils

Directions:
Give students directions according to the type of list you want them to make.

Prewriting Idea List
Brainstorm a list of ideas on a current writing topic. Use the list to generate ideas for the writing piece.

"To Do" List
Create a "To Do" List for yourself, a story character, or a historical figure.

Safety Checklist

Make a checklist of important home safety rules. Use the list to do a safety check.

Shopping List

Create a shopping list for yourself or for someone from another time or culture.

Problem-Solving List

Make a list of possible solutions to a problem. Prioritize the items on the list.

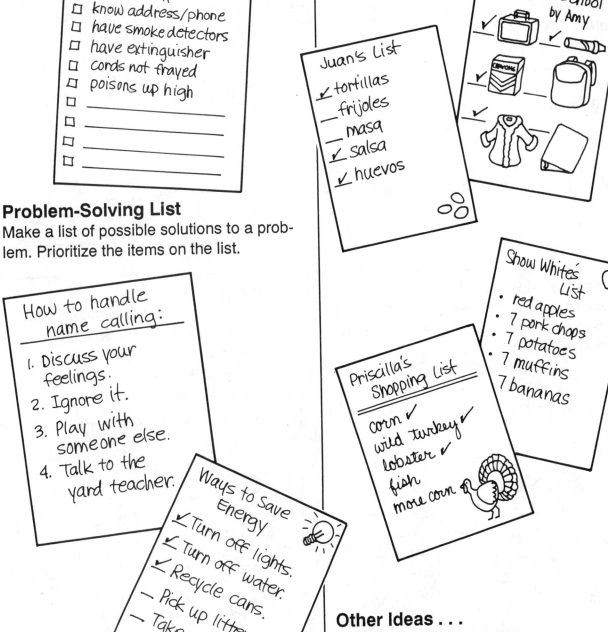

Safety Checklist ✔
☐ can call 911
☐ know address/phone
☐ have smoke detectors
☐ have extinguisher
☐ cords not frayed
☐ poisons up high
☐ _____
☐ _____
☐ _____
☐ _____

How to handle name calling:
1. Discuss your feelings.
2. Ignore it.
3. Play with someone else.
4. Talk to the yard teacher.

Ways to Save Energy
✔ Turn off lights.
✔ Turn off water.
✔ Recycle cans.
— Pick up litter.
— Take short showers.

Juan's List
✔ tortillas
— frijoles
— masa
✔ salsa
✔ huevos

Shopping for School by Amy

Priscilla's Shopping List
corn ✔
wild turkey ✔
lobster ✔
fish
more corn

Show White's List
• red apples
• 7 pork chops
• 7 potatoes
• 7 muffins
7 bananas

Other Ideas . . .
- Compare/contrast list
- List of facts learned
- Valentine list
- List poem
- List of attributes

Maps

To design a map, students must use math skills, organize information, and show an understanding of directionality. Mapping is a good activity for partners or small groups.

Materials:
- plain paper
- rulers
- pencils
- crayons/markers

Directions:
After giving the class background knowledge about maps and opportunities to read different kinds of maps, have students make their own maps for the theme being studied.

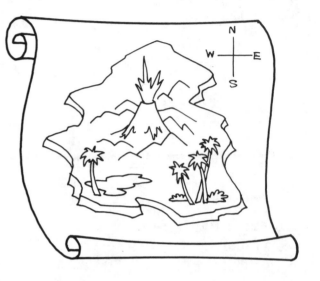

Historical Map

Make a map showing the route of a historical figure or group. Write a description of the trip and attach it to the back of the map.

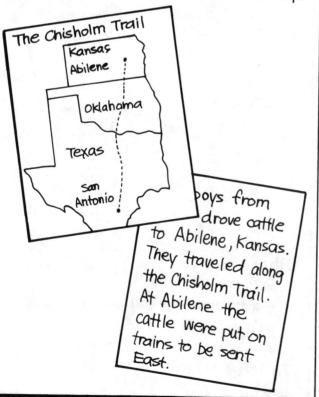

Math Map

Use selected math facts to make a map that guides a traveler from *Start* to *Finish*. Trade maps with a classmate, solve the problems, and write about the journey.

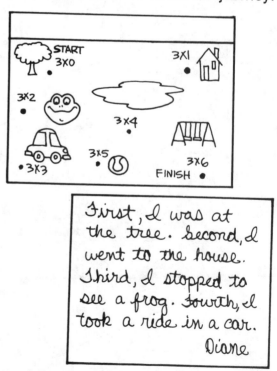

Personal Map

Make a map of a room in your house and describe the setting on the back.

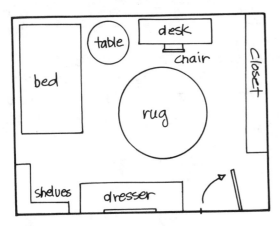

School Map

Show the layout of your classroom or school on a map. Describe it on the back.

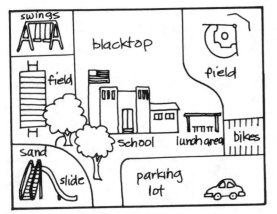

Social Science Map

Draw a map of your city or neighborhood. Label the map with the names of streets, buildings, and landmarks.

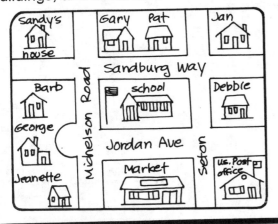

Literature Map

Show the travels of a book character by making a map of the places visited. Write about the character's adventures on the back of the map or on another piece of paper.

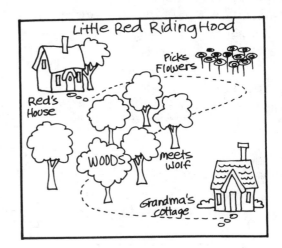

Make a map showing the setting of a favorite story. Write about the setting on the back.

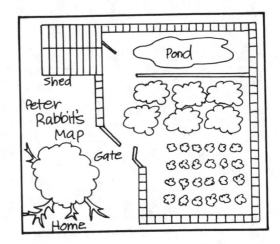

Other Ideas . . .

- Treasure map
- Imaginary adventure map
- Road map
- Scavenger hunt map

Mobiles

Mobile activities spark creativity and provide another opportunity for students to write. A mobile is constructed around a theme and its parts reflect aspects of that theme. For younger children, the parts of a mobile can be as simple as drawings on index cards. Older children can do more detailed work.

Materials:
- assorted construction paper
- coat hangers or empty cardboard rolls
- index cards
- crayons/markers
- pencils
- yarn or string
- scissors
- glue

Directions:
Students create people or objects that represent the theme being studied, then write facts on the back of the pictures or on index cards. Attach the work to the hanger with yarn.

Literature Mobiles
Create a mobile showing the setting, main characters, or sequence of events in a favorite story.

Personal Attributes
Construct a mobile about yourself, a friend, or a family member. Include a drawing of the person and three or more statements that describe him/her.

Alternatives to Worksheets

Creative Teaching Press

Historical Figure

Select a historical figure and draw a portrait of that person for the top of the mobile. Illustrate and write about him/her and attach this information to the hanger.

Other Types of Mobiles

Mobiles can also be constructed with tagboard shapes or cardboard tubes and yarn.

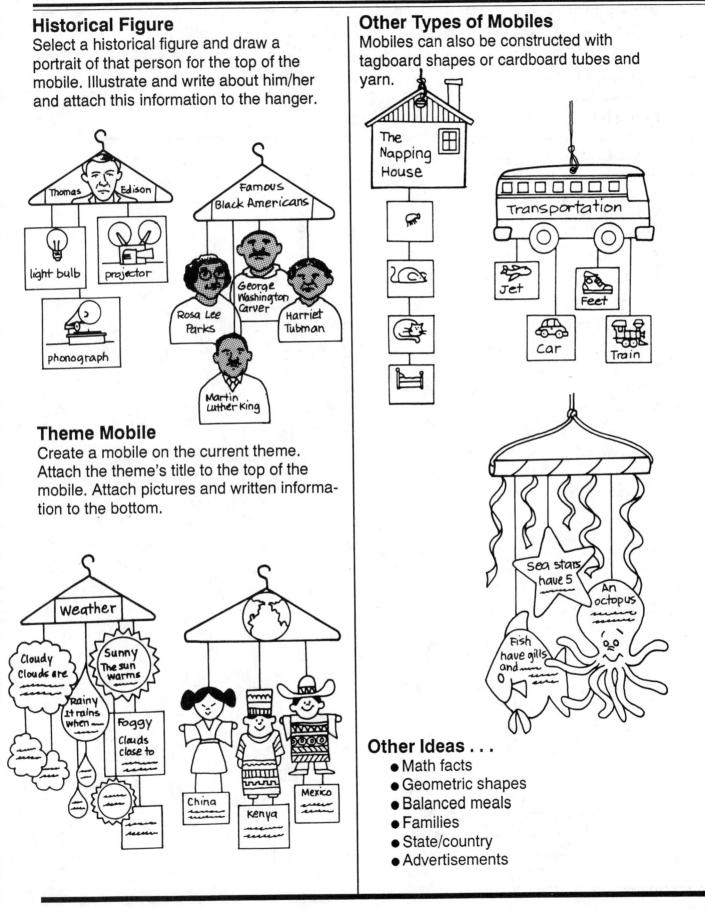

Theme Mobile

Create a mobile on the current theme. Attach the theme's title to the top of the mobile. Attach pictures and written information to the bottom.

Other Ideas . . .

- Math facts
- Geometric shapes
- Balanced meals
- Families
- State/country
- Advertisements

Paper Bag Activities

Versatile and inexpensive, paper bags can be used for many activities. Paper bags come in many sizes and can be cut apart, stuffed for a 3-D effect, made into hand puppets, or used as containers. When made to resemble hide, bark, or antique paper, paper bags provide an interesting textured surface for activities related to history, nature, and other cultures.

Materials:
- paper bags (assorted sizes)
- construction paper (assorted colors)
- crayons/markers
- pencils
- scissors
- glue and tape
- index cards or slips of paper

Directions:
Select a bag of the appropriate size and instruct students according to the project chosen. To make hide, bark, or antique paper, have students cut out one side of the bag, tear the edges, then crumple and straighten the paper several times to add texture.

Literature Sequencing
Decorate the bag to look like the setting or cover of a story the class has read. On index cards, describe the main events in the story, then place the cards in the bag. Trade bags with a classmate and sequence the story.

Riddle Bag
Select an object and place it in a bag. Write three clues about the object on the front of the bag. Trade bags with a classmate and solve each other's riddles.

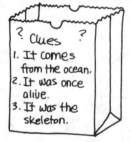

Theme Facts
Select objects related to the theme being studied or write and illustrate facts about the theme. Place the objects/facts in a decorated bag. Exchange bags with classmates for discussion, reading, and/or analysis.

Historical Letter

Write a letter from a historical figure that reflects the era in which he/she lived.

Pictographs

Tell a story in pictures, then write the story below the pictographs.

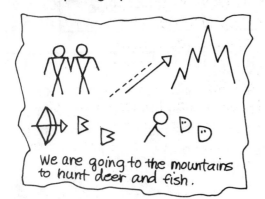

Ecology

Write about an ecological concern on a recyclable paper bag.

Book Character Report

Draw and cut out a picture of a book's main character. Attach it to the front of a large grocery bag. Write a report about the book and glue it to the back of the bag. Stuff the bag with newspaper and tape the top closed. Place the character in a chair or on a table.

Stuffed Bags

Decorate a bag to represent a topic being studied. Stuff the bag with newspaper and tie it with yarn. Write facts about your character on an index card, punch a hole in the card, and tie it to the bag.

Other Ideas . . .

- Paper bag puppets
- Survival bag
- Book jackets
- Proclamations
- Treasure map

Peek-overs and Add-ons

Peek-overs and add-ons, art projects related to the theme being studied, are added to student writing. These creative additions make especially appealing classroom displays.

Materials:
- writing paper
- construction paper
- glue
- scissors
- crayons/markers
- pencils
- butcher paper (for life-size picture)
- paint and brushes (for life-size picture)

Directions:
Direct students to write about the selected topic. Next, have them design an appropriate peek-over or add-on. Attach the art to the writing.

Science
After writing science facts, complete a peek-over/add-on to highlight the theme.

Self-concept
After painting a life-size self-portrait on butcher paper, write your autobiography and attach it to the picture. Include photographs if you choose.

Holidays/Seasons

Write about the current holiday or season and design an appropriate symbol to add to your writing.

Thanksgiving

I would not like to be a turkey on Thanksgiving.

Literature Responses

Summarize, respond to, or describe a favorite part of a book you have read. Attach an appropriate peek-over/add-on.

Strega Nona
by Tomie de Paola
Strega Nona had a pasta pot. She said magic words

Pigs
by Robert Munsch
"Hey, you dumb pigs!"
The pigs ran to the grocery store. They knocked over

The wheels on the bus go round and round. The people go up and down.

Famous People

Research and write about a famous person. Have the famous person peek over your report.

Daniel Boone

Daniel Boone was a frontiersman. He wore a

Sally Ride

Sally Ride was the first woman to go up in space.

George Washington

George Washington was the first president of the United States. He was a general in the

Other Ideas . . .

- Multicultural peek-over/add-on
- Mother's Day/Father's Day peek-over
- Friend peek-over
- Life-size book character
- Life-size famous person

Pennants and Banners

Pennants and banners add spirit to the delivery of a message. Students must be selective as they choose words that will encourage others or make a personal statement. On the back of the pennant/banner, students can elaborate on the message that appears on the front.

Materials:
- construction paper (for pennant)
- butcher/shelf paper (for banner)
- scissors
- glue
- crayons/markers
- pencils
- paint and brushes (optional)
- sticks (optional)

Directions:
Cut paper to the appropriate size and shape for a banner or pennant. Add sticks if desired.

Literature
Write the title of your favorite book on the front of a banner. On the back, tell more about the book.

Support a Cause
Encourage others to support a worthy cause. On the back of the banner tell why the cause is important.

Science
On a banner, write about what you are learning in science. Put the title or main idea on the front and give supporting details on the back.

Alternatives to Worksheets   Creative Teaching Press

Announce an Event

Make a pennant/banner advertising a special event. Explain the importance of the event on the back.

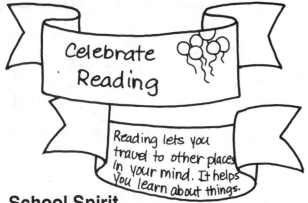

School Spirit

Design a pennant/banner that reflects school spirit. Write three facts about your school on the back.

Class Banner

Working with a partner, make a banner to place at the entrance to the classroom. Write a description of the class on the back of the banner. (Note: Change the banners throughout the year so that every student's work is displayed.)

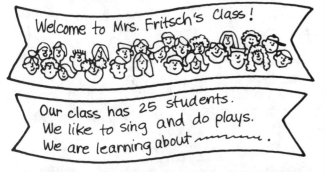

Historical Figure

Cheer on a historical figure by creating a banner celebrating his/her importance. Explain the banner's significance on the back.

Congratulatory Banner

Create a banner congratulating a fictional character or a real person.

Other Ideas . . .

- Self-concept banner
- State banner
- Holiday pennant
- Political pennant

Pop-ups

Pop-ups add action and an element of surprise to writing activities. Pop-up projects can be one page or a multipage book. Children love pop-ups and will read them again and again.

Materials:
- construction paper (9" x 12" or 12" x 18")
- pencils
- scissors
- glue
- crayons/markers
- writing paper (optional)

Directions:
Fold a sheet of construction paper in half. Make a tab by cutting two slits on the fold, one inch apart. Push the tab through to the inside. Draw, color, and cut out a figure that will not extend beyond the book page. Glue the figure to the tab.

Story Sequence
Show the beginning, middle, and end of a story by making a three-page pop-up book. Include a written description of the main events.

Award
Make a pop-up award for someone you admire. The recipient can be a historical figure, a book character, or someone you know.

Story Setting
Re-create the setting of a story. Cut additional tabs if needed. Describe the setting in writing at the bottom of the pop-up.

Riddles
Write clues on the front of the pop-up page. The answer should pop up when the book is opened.

Alternatives to Worksheets   Creative Teaching Press

Life Cycle

Show each stage in the life cycle of an animal on a separate page of a pop-up book.

Greeting Cards

Celebrate a special day by surprising a friend with a pop-up card.

Math

Select a number for your pop-up and write as many facts as you can for that number.

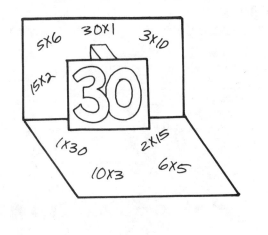

Theme Unit

On pop-up pages, write and illustrate facts learned during a theme unit. Assemble the pages into an individual or a class book.

Self-concept

Make a pop-up page showing yourself doing something you do well. The pages can be glued together for a class book titled "We Are All Special."

Other Ideas . . .

- Poems
- Jokes
- Story characters
- Mystery questions

Postcards and Telegrams

Postcards and telegrams give students an opportunity to communicate by writing clear, concise messages. Students can write from their own perspective or that of others. Like all correspondence, postcards and telegrams should be shared with others.

Materials:
- large index cards (5" x 8")
- crayons/markers
- pencils

Directions:
First, model the correct format of a post-card or telegram. Have students complete their work on index cards, using the layout you have selected. For picture postcards, add an illustration on the back of the card.

Historygram
Write about an important historical event. Use accurate and timely information.

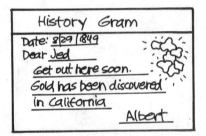

Storygram
Write an urgent message to a book charac-ter. The message can be from you or from one story character to another.

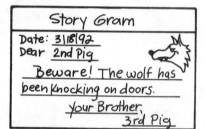

Happygram
Write a message that will make a family member, friend, or classmate feel happy and good about himself.

Sciencegram
Write a brief factual message about a scientific discovery or observation. Be sure to include the date of the discovery.

Science Postcard

Put yourself in another environment—under the sea, out in space, in a rain forest—and write about what happens to you. Base your adventures on scientific fact. Illustrate your message.

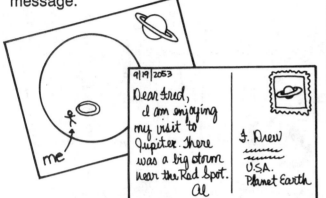

Book Character Postcard

Write a postcard from one story character to another. The message should be based on events in the story.

History Postcard

Take on the role of a historical figure and write a postcard that reflects your time and place in history.

Travel Postcard

Pretend to visit another state or country, and write about your trip. On one side of the card, draw something you have seen in your travels.

Family Postcard

Write to your family telling them about something you are learning in school.

Other Ideas . . .

- Congratulations telegram
- Singing telegram
- Holiday postcard
- Postcard order form

Posters and Ads

Posters and ads require students to recall information and condense what they have learned into a few carefully chosen words. On the back of the poster/ad students can write more about the topic.

Materials:
- construction paper (12" x 18")
- crayons/markers
- pencils
- paper scraps (optional)

Directions:
After displaying and discussing posters/ads, instruct students to create a poster or ad on the selected topic.

Historical Ad
Pretend to be someone from the past and develop an ad reflecting the time period in which you live. Write an explanation of the ad on the back.

Personal Poster
Create a poster about yourself, a friend, or a family member. On the back of the poster, tell what makes this person special.

Literature Poster/Ad

Design a poster/ad that highlights a story character or plot. Tell more about the subject on the back.

Health/Safety Poster

Design a poster promoting good health or safety. Explain the importance of the message on the back.

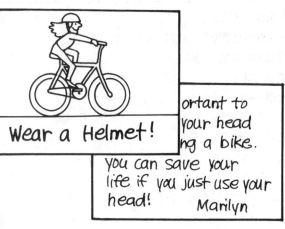

Product Ad

Invent a product and write an ad to sell it.

Other Ideas . . .

- Ecology poster
- Political poster
- School/class poster
- Event poster
- Theme poster

Puzzles

By working puzzles, children improve visual discrimination and spatial relationship skills. When students create their own puzzles, they learn to think creatively. Writing should be incorporated into the puzzle whenever possible. Puzzles can be reassembled using the picture side or the story side.

Materials:
- construction paper or tagboard
- crayons/markers
- pencils
- scissors
- envelopes or plastic storage bags

Directions:
Students create a picture according to the project selected. Next, they write on the back of the picture and cut it into large pieces. Store the puzzle pieces in envelopes or plastic bags.

Theme-Related Puzzles
Illustrate and write about facts learned in a current theme unit. Cut the puzzle apart and trade the pieces with a classmate for reassembly.

Shape Puzzles
Make puzzles in the shape of an object.

Puzzling Message

Write a message and cut it apart. Place the pieces in an envelope and mail it or give it to a friend.

Literature Puzzles

Draw the setting and the main characters of a story. Write about the story on the back. Make your work into a puzzle for others to reassemble.

Partner Puzzles

Work with a partner to create a puzzle on the assigned topic. Draw a picture and cut it into puzzle pieces. Write a clue or fact about the picture on the back of each piece.

Self-concept Puzzle

Write your name and draw a self-portrait on one side of the paper. Write facts about yourself on the other side. Cut the portrait apart to make a puzzle.

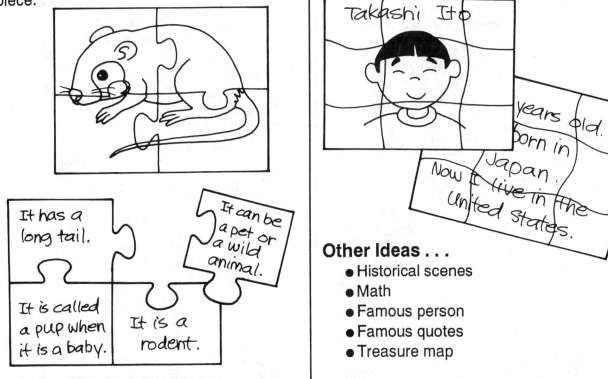

Other Ideas . . .

- Historical scenes
- Math
- Famous person
- Famous quotes
- Treasure map

Quilts

Quilt-making challenges students to think about what they have learned and come up with multiple ideas about a topic. Quilts make attractive bulletin board displays and wall hangings.

Materials:
- construction paper squares
  (approx. 6" x 6") or quilt pattern, p. 93
- butcher paper (for quilt backing)
- crayons/markers
- pencils
- glue

Directions:

Class Quilt: Each student designs one quilt square on a common theme. Mount the completed squares on a bulletin board or on butcher paper to form a large quilt. Add "stitches" with a crayon or marking pen.

Individual Quilt: Give each student the appropriate number of squares and specific directions. Glue the completed squares on a large sheet of paper. Add "stitches" with a crayon or a marking pen.

Self-concept
Design a square or squares that tell about you.

Theme
Create a square or squares that show what you have learned about a theme you are studying.

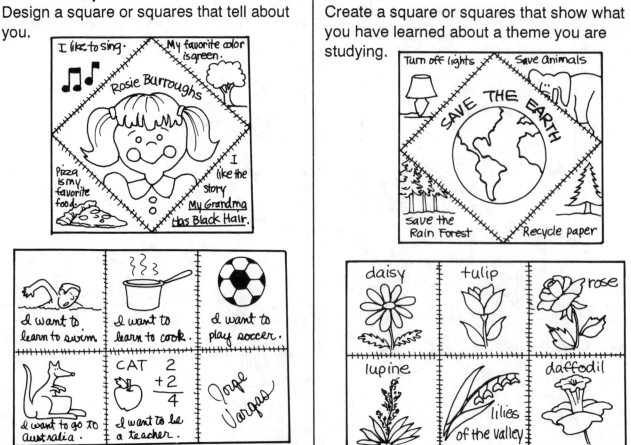

Literature

Design a square for a class quilt that tells about your favorite book.

Use six squares to illustrate and tell the sequence of events in a story. Put the squares together to form a quilt.

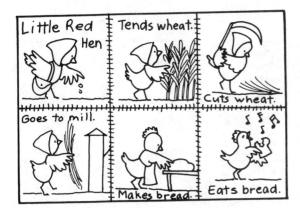

In each square write the title of a book you have read and add an illustration. Join the squares to make a book quilt.

Math

Design a quilt square that shows what you are studying in math (patterning, geometric shapes, numbers, fractions).

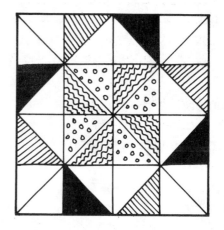

Famous People

Make a square for a class quilt depicting famous people and their contributions.

Other Ideas . . .

- Story elements
- Name quilt
- Memory quilt
- State quilt

Recipes, Menus, and Prescriptions

Developing and writing real or imaginary recipes and prescriptions gets students thinking logically and creatively. Students should include all the necessary ingredients and give concise sequential directions. Students can also research a topic and synthesize information to create an appropriate menu.

Materials:
- large index card or pattern, p. 94 (for recipe)
- lined paper or pattern, p. 95 (for prescription)
- construction paper (for menu)
- crayons/markers
- pencils

Directions:
Prepare appropriate paper for the project. Direct students to write a recipe, prescription, or menu related to the topic selected.

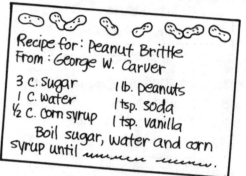

Recipe for: Peanut Brittle
From: George W. Carver

3 c. sugar   1 lb. peanuts
1 c. water   1 tsp. soda
½ c. corn syrup 1 tsp. vanilla
    Boil sugar, water and corn syrup until ‿‿‿‿ ‿‿‿‿.

Historical Recipe/Menu
Write a recipe that reflects your knowledge of a historical figure or a period in history.

Book Character Recipe/Menu/Prescription
Develop a recipe or a menu that reflects the tastes and personality of a book character.

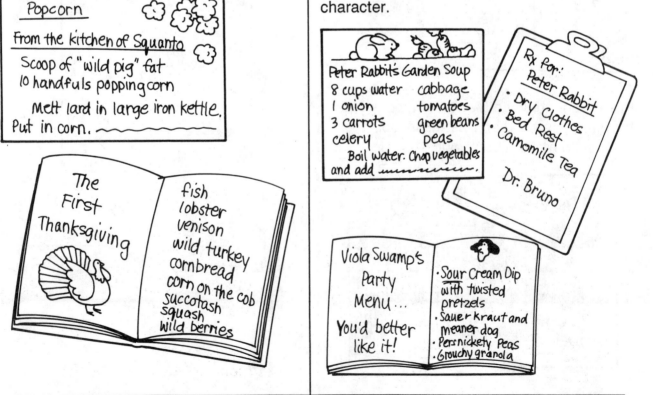

Popcorn

From the kitchen of Squanto
Scoop of "wild pig" fat
10 handfuls popping corn

    Melt lard in large iron kettle.
Put in corn. ‿‿‿‿

The First Thanksgiving

fish
lobster
venison
wild turkey
cornbread
corn on the cob
succotash
squash
wild berries

Peter Rabbit's Garden Soup
8 cups water   cabbage
1 onion   tomatoes
3 carrots   green beans
celery   peas
    Boil water. Chop vegetables and add ‿‿‿‿.

Rx For:
Peter Rabbit
• Dry Clothes
• Bed Rest
• Camomile Tea

Dr. Bruno

Viola Swamp's Party Menu...
You'd better like it!

• Sour Cream Dip with twisted pretzels
• Sauer kraut and meaner dog
• Persnickety Peas
• Grouchy granola

Recipe for a Special Day

Create a real or an imaginary recipe for a holiday or special day.

Recipe for: Mother's Day
From: Aaron   Serves 1
Ingredients:
1 c. love   3 smiles
2 hugs   ton of patience
1 kiss
     Stir ingredients together
to make world's best mom.

Theme Recipe

Invent a recipe that reflects the theme you are studying.

Mouse Muffins

muffins   1 candy corn
frosting   licorice string
2 raisins   2 round cookies
Frost the muffins, add cookie
ears, raisin eyes, ~~~~~~~.

"How To" Recipe/Prescription

Write a recipe or prescription that clearly describes the steps necessary to accomplish a task.

Recipe to
Ride a Bike
Ingredients:
• Balance
• Patience
• Confidence
• Helpful friend
Directions:
Have helpful friend
help you balance.
Take off. Try again
and again.

Rx for Good Day
• Sleep well.
• Eat good food.
• Read a book.
• Play with a
  friend.
• Do a kindness
  for someone.
• Smile a lot.
Dr. Drew

Dictated Recipe (younger students)

Dictate the recipe for your favorite dish and draw a picture of it.

Mmm good!

Oven Chicken
1. Wash chicken without feathers.
2. Put a cup of salt on it.
3. Bake it at 5° for 3 minutes.
4. Take it out. Eat it!

Cultural Recipe/Menu

After studying a different culture, use information you have learned to write an ethnic recipe or menu.

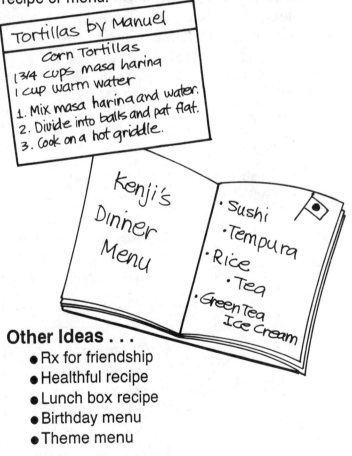

Tortillas by Manuel
   Corn Tortillas
1 3/4 cups masa harina
1 cup warm water
1. Mix masa harina and water.
2. Divide into balls and pat flat.
3. Cook on a hot griddle.

Kenji's Dinner Menu
• Sushi
• Tempura
• Rice
• Tea
• Green Tea Ice Cream

Other Ideas . . .

- Rx for friendship
- Healthful recipe
- Lunch box recipe
- Birthday menu
- Theme menu

Rules

Children enjoy making rules for *others* to follow. It makes them feel that they are in charge and encourages them to think and write clearly, concisely, and realistically.

Materials:
- construction paper (12" x 18")
- crayons/markers
- pencils
- scissors (optional)
- glue (optional)

Directions:
After discussing rules and their purpose, have students develop and write rules based on the selected topic.

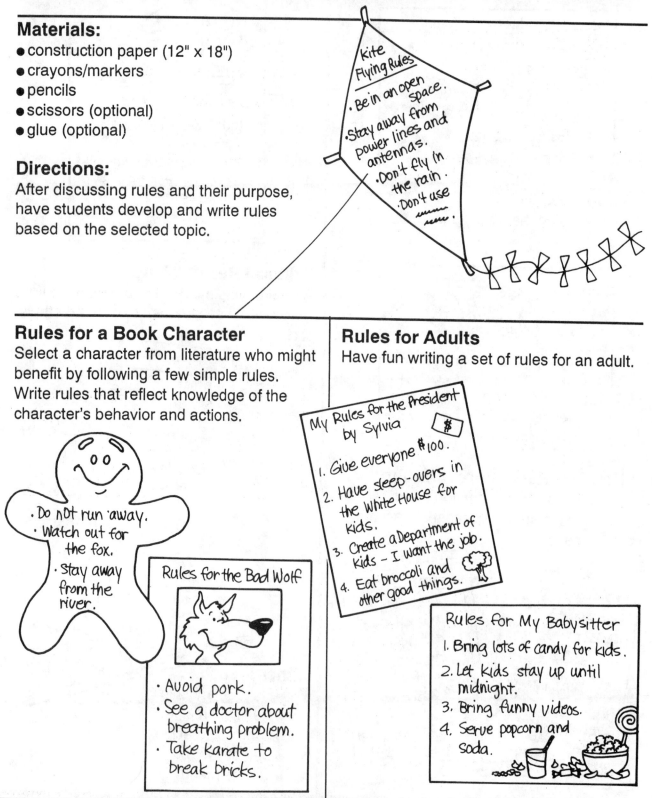

Kite Flying Rules
- Be in an open space.
- Stay away from power lines and antennas.
- Don't fly in the rain.
- Don't use ___.

Rules for a Book Character
Select a character from literature who might benefit by following a few simple rules. Write rules that reflect knowledge of the character's behavior and actions.

- Do not run away.
- Watch out for the fox.
- Stay away from the river.

Rules for the Bad Wolf
- Avoid pork.
- See a doctor about breathing problem.
- Take karate to break bricks.

Rules for Adults
Have fun writing a set of rules for an adult.

My Rules for the President
by Sylvia
1. Give everyone $100.
2. Have sleep-overs in the White House for kids.
3. Create a Department of Kids — I want the job.
4. Eat broccoli and other good things.

Rules for My Babysitter
1. Bring lots of candy for kids.
2. Let kids stay up until midnight.
3. Bring funny videos.
4. Serve popcorn and soda.

Alternatives to Worksheets

Creative Teaching Press

Classroom/School Rules

Make your own set of rules for appropriate school/classroom behavior. Share your rules with the class.

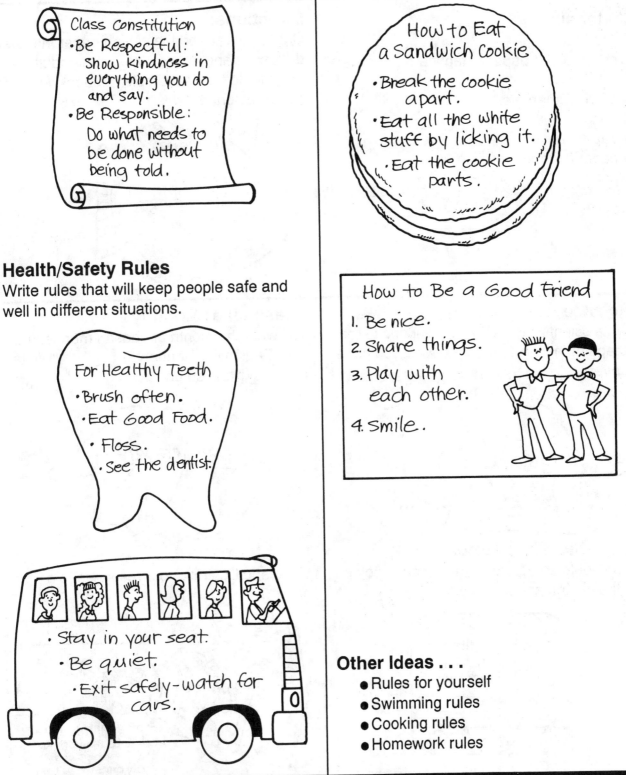

Class Constitution
- Be Respectful: Show kindness in everything you do and say.
- Be Responsible: Do what needs to be done without being told.

Health/Safety Rules

Write rules that will keep people safe and well in different situations.

For Healthy Teeth
- Brush often.
- Eat Good Food.
- Floss.
- See the dentist.

- Stay in your seat.
- Be quiet.
- Exit safely—watch for cars.

"How To" Rules

Choose a specific activity and write rules that explain how to do it successfully.

How to Eat a Sandwich Cookie
- Break the cookie apart.
- Eat all the white stuff by licking it.
- Eat the cookie parts.

How to Be a Good Friend
1. Be nice.
2. Share things.
3. Play with each other.
4. Smile.

Other Ideas . . .
- Rules for yourself
- Swimming rules
- Cooking rules
- Homework rules

Shape Books

Children like to write on paper cut into unusual shapes. Use shape books to motivate student writing and to create class books. Shape books adapt equally well to a Big Book format and small-scale individual projects.

Materials:
- lined paper
- construction paper or tagboard (for cover)
- scissors
- crayons/markers
- pencils
- paper punch
- paper fasteners or yarn
- pattern, p. 92 (for person book)

Directions:
Cut the cover and the writing paper into the desired shape. In most cases, an adult will need to do this. Assemble the book with paper fasteners or yarn.

Science
Write scientific facts that correspond to the shape of the book. Illustrate what you have written.

Seasonal or Monthly
Tell what the month or season means to you. Begin with "January is _____," "Winter is _____," and so on.

Thematic Shape Book
Contribute a page to a class shape book on a theme you are studying.

Literature
Write and illustrate your response to a story.

Alternatives to Worksheets Creative Teaching Press

Special Event

Write about your participation in a special event. Illustrate what you have written.

THE JOG-A-THON

Colors

Write about and draw objects that are the same color as the book cover.

Red

Red is hearts and apples and a rose and a red hot candy!

Geometric Shape Books

Draw and label pictures of objects made with the geometric shape featured on the book cover.

A Book of Triangles

A witch hat is a triangle.

Field Trips

Write about a field trip in a book shaped to reflect the experience.

Our Trip to the Dairy

Our Trip to the Poultry Farm

Person Shape Book

Using the person pattern on page 92 or a pattern of your own, make a book cover depicting a historical figure, community worker, friend, or yourself. Write about the person represented on the cover of the book.

Community Helpers

The mail carrier delivers letters to my house. He works at the post office.

Other Ideas . . .
- Holidays
- Book character
- Number shape

Triaramas and Quadraramas

Triaramas are a three-dimensional way for students to display what they have learned. Four triaramas can be glued together to form a quadrarama.

Materials:

- construction paper (9" x 9")
- construction paper scraps
- glue
- scissors
- crayons/markers
- pencils

Directions:

1. Fold the top right corner of the square down to the lower left corner. Repeat with the opposite corners.
2. Open and cut one fold line to the center of the square.
3. Draw a background scene on half the square as shown.
4. Overlap the two bottom triangles and glue. Add stand-up parts to complete the triarama.

Science

On a triarama, illustrate and write about what you have learned during a current unit of study.

THE DESERT

Illustrate and write about science concepts on a four-part quadrarama. Glue the four sections together and display the quadrarama on a table or hang it from the ceiling with yarn.

It hatches in 21 days.

Social Science

Use a triarama to show your knowledge of people, places, and events. Write about what you have learned on the back.

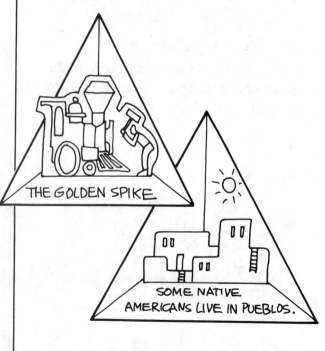

THE GOLDEN SPIKE

SOME NATIVE AMERICANS LIVE IN PUEBLOS.

Alternatives to Worksheets

Creative Teaching Press

Literature

Make a triarama representing the setting and characters of a story you have read. Before you set up the triarama, write about your display on the back.

On a quadrarama, show and write about the sequence of important events in a story.

Create a quadrarama representing four different books written by the same author. Label each part with a book title.

Self-concept

Draw and write about yourself and/or your family on a triarama.

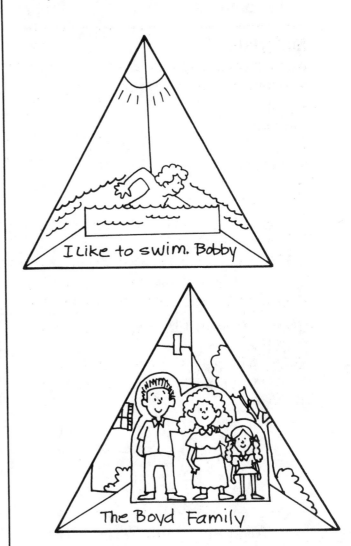

Other Ideas . . .

- Favorite nursery rhymes/poems/songs
- Other cultures
- Chronology of events
- Biography of a famous person

Venn Diagrams

Venn diagrams are ideal for comparing and contrasting two or more topics. After completing many Venn diagrams as a whole group activity, have students complete the charts alone or with a partner. Venn diagrams can be used to write compare/contrast paragraphs.

Materials:
- paper
- pencils

Directions:
Have students draw two overlapping circles. Instruct students to compare two topics by listing differences on the left and right and similarities in the center.

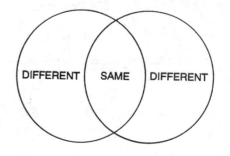

Characters in Literature
Select two characters from a story and compare them.

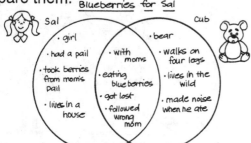

Two Books on the Same Theme
Read two books on the same theme and compare them.

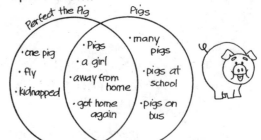

Two Versions of the Same Story
Read versions of the same story by two different authors. Use the Venn diagram to show the similarities and differences.

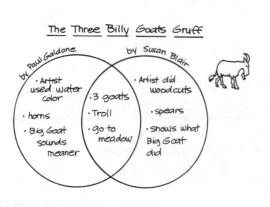

Comparing Cultures
Compare a story from your culture with a similar one from another culture.

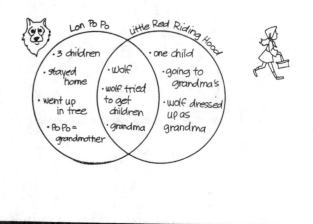

Alternatives to Worksheets
Creative Teaching Press

Looking for Attributes

Use a Venn diagram to show attributes of persons, places, or things.

Other Venn Diagram Formats

Compare three items by overlapping three circles. The center section is for traits common to all three.

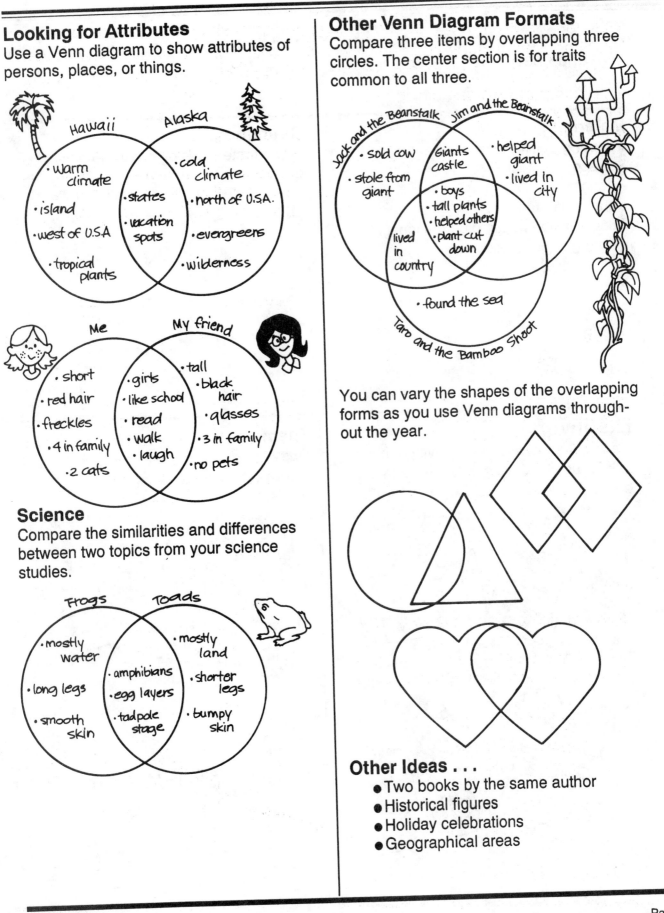

Hawaii / Alaska

- warm climate
- island
- west of U.S.A
- tropical plants
- states
- vacation spots
- cold climate
- north of U.S.A.
- evergreens
- wilderness

Me / My friend

- short
- red hair
- freckles
- 4 in family
- 2 cats
- girls
- like school
- read
- walk
- laugh
- tall
- black hair
- glasses
- 3 in family
- no pets

Science

Compare the similarities and differences between two topics from your science studies.

Frogs / Toads

- mostly water
- long legs
- smooth skin
- amphibians
- egg layers
- tadpole stage
- mostly land
- shorter legs
- bumpy skin

Jack and the Beanstalk / Jim and the Beanstalk / Taro and the Bamboo Shoot

- sold cow
- stole from giant
- Giants castle
- helped giant
- lived in city
- boys
- tall plants
- helped others
- plant cut down
- lived in country
- found the sea

You can vary the shapes of the overlapping forms as you use Venn diagrams throughout the year.

Other Ideas . . .

- Two books by the same author
- Historical figures
- Holiday celebrations
- Geographical areas

Vests

A paper bag vest allows students to show off their work by wearing it. Inexpensive and easy to acquire, paper bags provide a good surface for drawing or writing.

Materials:
- paper grocery bag
- scissors
- pencils
- crayons/markers
- construction paper, glue (optional)
- writing paper (optional)

Directions:
Pop out the sides of the bag and lay it flat. Cut as shown.

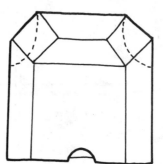

BACK

FRONT

Literature
Make a vest to wear when giving a book talk, or use the vest to advertise a favorite book.

Theme
Use a vest to promote a cause or display something you have learned.

Alternatives to Worksheets

Creative Teaching Press

Math Patterning

Glue or draw shapes of various colors in a repeated pattern around the edge of the vest.

Self-concept

Design an illustrated vest that tells others about you. Wear the vest as you introduce yourself to the class.

Famous Person

Choose a famous person you admire and make a vest informing others of this person's contributions.

Careers

Create a vest for a specific occupation. Wear your vest and tell the class about the occupation, or write about it and paste your report on the back of the vest.

Other Ideas . . .

- Cultural costumes
- Historical costumes
- Drama costumes
- Autograph vest

Visors

Visors allow students to display their work by wearing it. More complex visors can be made by adding parts.

Materials:
- construction paper or tagboard
- visor pattern, p. 96
- crayons/markers
- scissors
- pencils
- 15" x 1" paper strip
- stapler
- construction paper scraps (optional)

Directions:
Reproduce the visor pattern on tagboard. Cut out, decorate, and write on the visor. Staple on a paper strip.

Literature
Encourage a friend to read your favorite book by advertising it on your visor.

Theme Visor
Make a visor inspired by a current unit of study.

Patriotic Visor
Design a patriotic visor with a red, white, and blue design. Write a fact about the U.S.A. on the back of the visor.

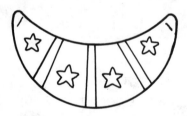

Name Visor
Use markers to write your name on the visor in fancy colorful letters. Next, draw a picture of yourself or a design that reflects something you like to do. Write about yourself on the back of the visor.

Alternatives to Worksheets

Creative Teaching Press

Phonics Visor

Write a letter in the center of the visor. Decorate your visor by drawing pictures that begin with the letter's is sound. Wear the visor on a "sound hunt."

Sun Visor

Decorate a visor in warm colors. Write tips about staying healthy in the sun.

Animal Visor

Make your visor look like an animal from literature or science, and write about it on the underside of the visor.

3-D Visor

Use construction paper parts to add personality to your visor.

Other Ideas . . .

- Careers visor
- Book character visor
- Field trip visor
- Report visor

Award Pattern

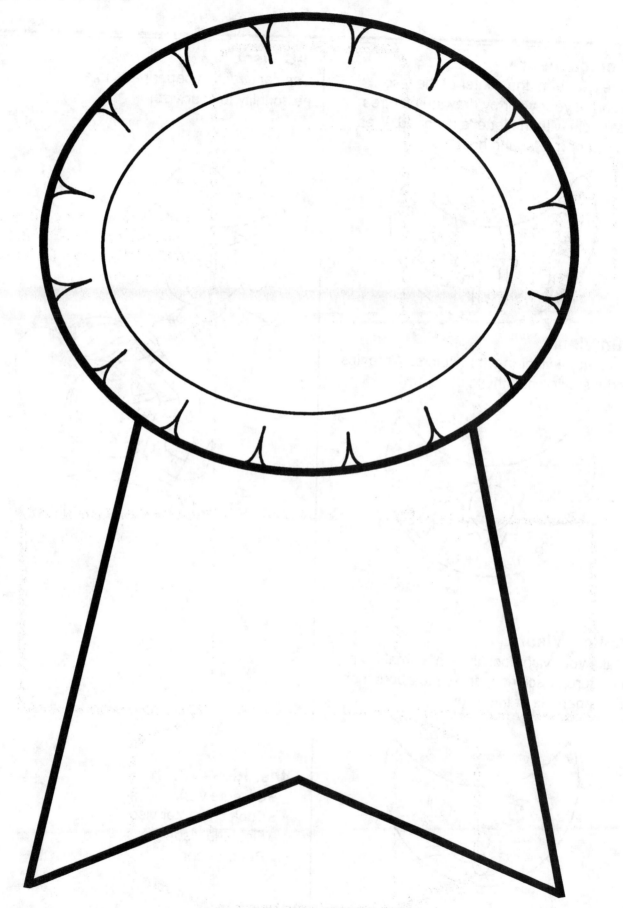

Alternatives to Worksheets

Creative Teaching Press

Cube Pattern

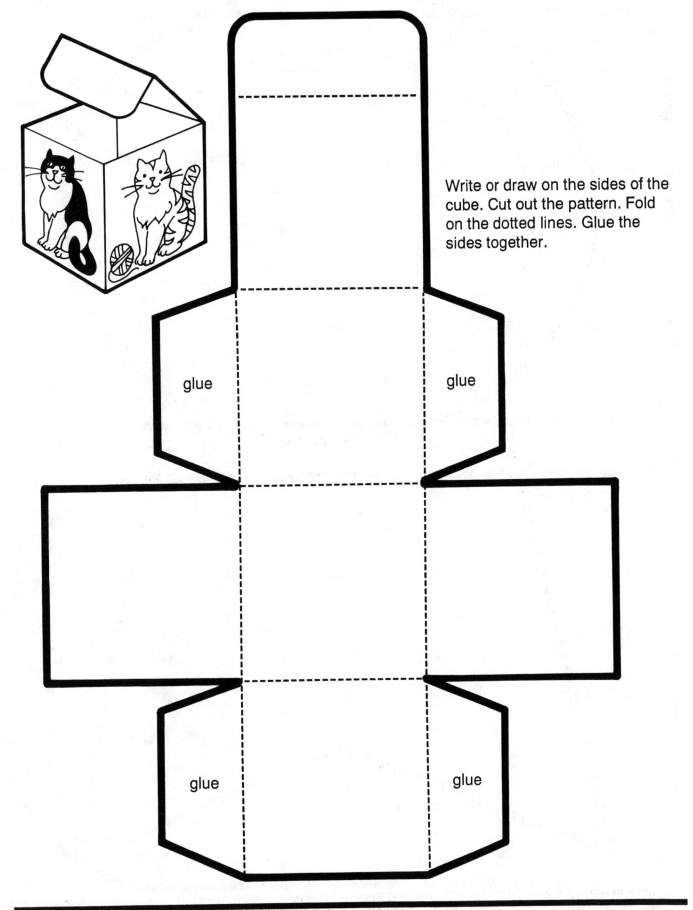

Write or draw on the sides of the cube. Cut out the pattern. Fold on the dotted lines. Glue the sides together.

glue

glue

glue

glue

Door Hanger Pattern

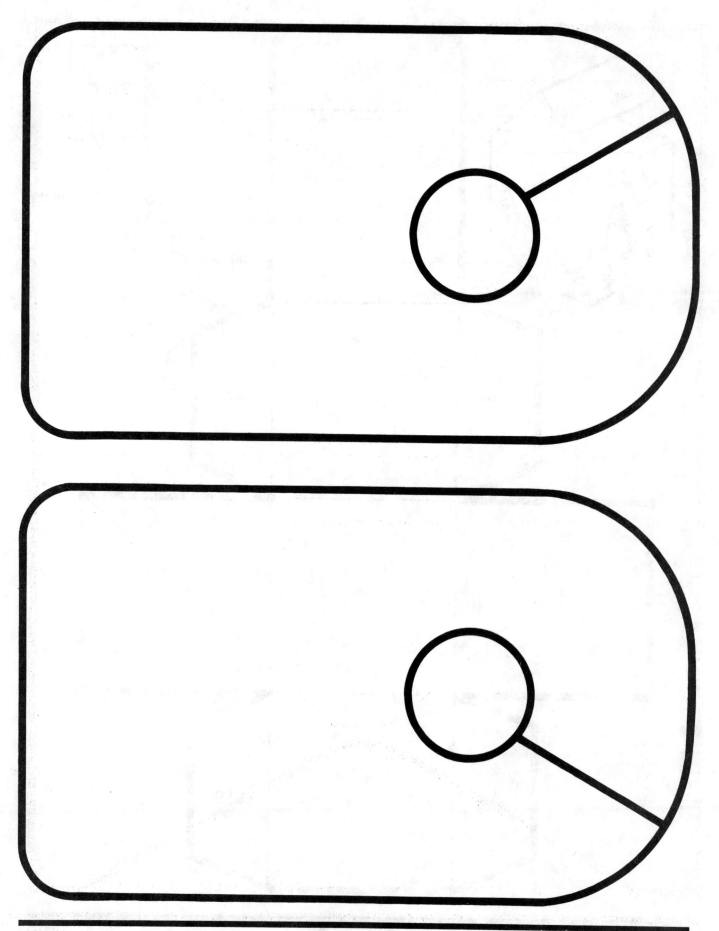

Alternatives to Worksheets

Creative Teaching Press

fold

Stamp

Stamp Pattern

Pop-up Card

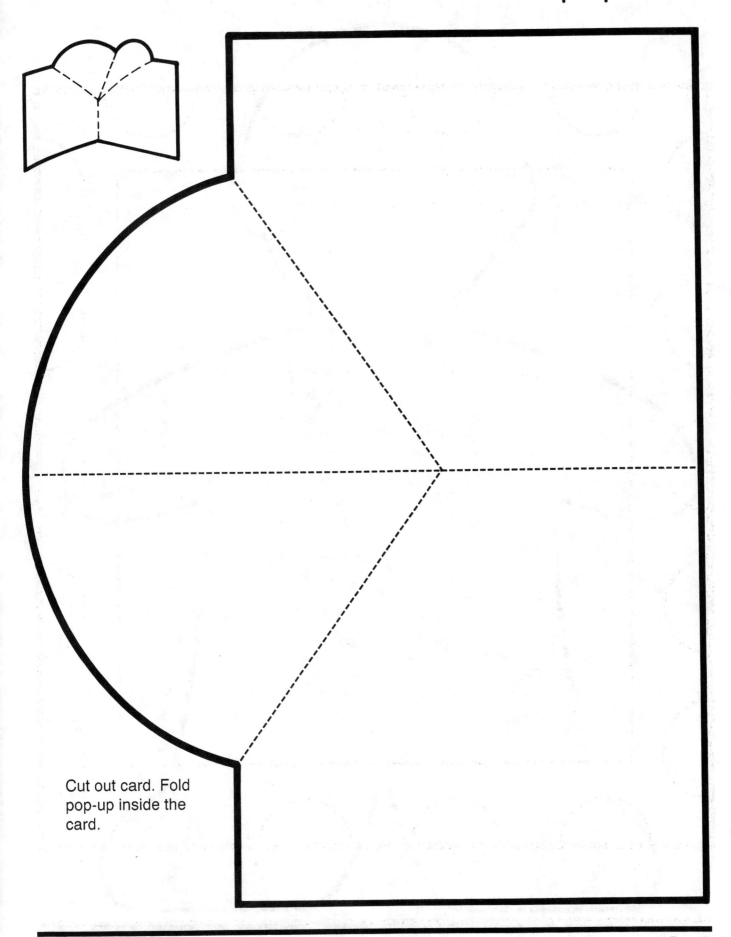

Cut out card. Fold pop-up inside the card.

People Flaps/Person Shape Book Pattern

Alternatives to Worksheets

Creative Teaching Press

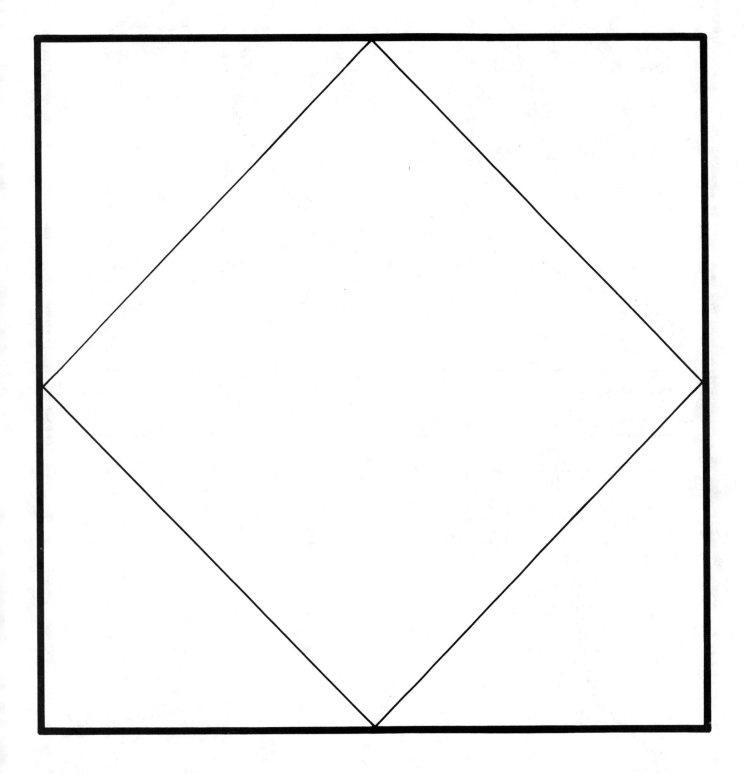

Recipe Card

_____ 's

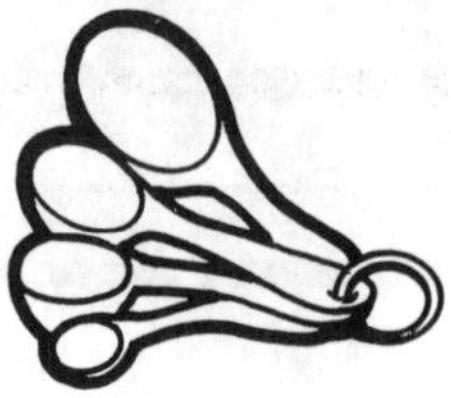

Recipe for_____

Number of servings: _____

Ingredients:

_____ _____

_____ _____

_____ _____

_____ _____

- -

Directions:

_____

_____

_____

_____

_____

_____

_____

_____

_____

Alternatives to Worksheets

Creative Teaching Press

R℞

Doctor _____ 's Prescription

for _____

_____

_____

_____

_____

_____

_____

_____

Visor Pattern

Cut out and decorate.
Staple on a paper strip.